WOMEN AND WORSHIP AT CORINTH

Women and Worship at
CORINTH

Paul's Rhetorical Arguments
in 1 Corinthians

Lucy Peppiatt

CASCADE *Books* · Eugene, Oregon

WOMEN AND WORSHIP AT CORINTH
Paul's Rhetorical Arguments in 1 Corinthians

Cascade Books
An Imprint of Wipf and Stock Publishers
199 W. 8th Ave., Suite 3
Eugene, OR 97401

www.wipfandstock.com

ISBN 13: 978-1-4982-0146-9

Cataloging-in-Publication data:

Peppiatt, Lucy.

    Women and worship at Corinth / Lucy Peppiatt, with a foreword by Douglas Campbell.

    xii + 148 p.; 23 cm—Includes bibliographical references and index.

    ISBN 13: 978-1-4982-0146-9

    1. Bible. Corinthians, 1st—Criticism, interpretation. 2. Women—Religious aspects—Christianity. 3. Bible, Epistles of Paul—Criticism, interpretation, etc. 4. Equality—Biblical teaching. I. Campbell, Douglas Atchinson, 1961–. II. Title.

BS2675.52 P362 2015

Manufactured in the USA.

For my parents, Hugh and Claire Peppiatt

Table of Contents

Foreword

The complex and contested Corinthian situation prompted Paul to address the role of women in the community's worship at some length in his first extant letter to that community, principally in 1 Cor 11:2–16 and, much more briefly, in 14:33–35. Needless to say, these discussions have subsequently become critical points of reference as the church has pivoted in the modern era to reevaluate its understanding of gender, along with its implications. But the reconstruction of the original sense of ancient texts is always a fraught business, and is, in addition, difficult to disentangle from the concerns and locations of the modern scholars undertaking the reconstruction. Hence I view Lucy Peppiatt's attempt to reinterpret these texts here in a way that is more sensitive to a live ongoing debate at Corinth, with the voices of the women themselves being seen in the text and thereby heard, as both bold and significant (so here she stands—to a degree—in the same interpretative trajectory as Antoinette Clark Wire's provocative work[1]).

Methodologically, this is a step beyond a rather flat account of Paul's text that is too strongly influenced by the tacit view that he is pronouncing himself in all his texts for posterity. I do not deny of course that his texts are important for posterity, but they were written in a unique way within the NT that we tend to lose touch with, namely, as fundamentally occasional, and hence lively, interactions with other, at times cantankerous, points of view. So I view Peppiatt's work as an important recovery of this dimension within their original production. Scholars frequently pay lip service to this dimension, but Peppiatt is really developing it. This is where her reading "lives," and, as a result, it is a lively, dramatic, gritty account.

1. *The Corinthian Women Prophets: A Reconstruction through Paul's Rhetoric* (Minneapolis: Fortress, 1990).

However, this book is an important methodological step forward in another respect. Peppiatt brings training in theology and argumentation to bear on the analysis of Paul. New Testament scholars are at times embarrassingly weak in these disciplines, which are actually critical for good exegetical work. Paul crafts arguments, generally in theological terms, and their assessment is therefore an important part of broader interpretation. So it is important to challenge the New Testament guild with scholarship and readings that are more sophisticated in terms of the actual argumentative issues, and Peppiatt does so. The result is an especially distinctive and helpful contribution to the broader exegetical discussion (at which point she is rather distinct from Wire's work, and similar treatments). Peppiatt's purview is theologically informed and argumentatively sensitive, but also deeply constructive.

At the end of the day, I suspect that Peppiatt's conclusions will be controversial. Not everyone will react well to her suggestions, and I have no doubt that she will be the target of criticism. But in my experience, much of this can be the proverbial heat not light, thrown off by defenders of readings that undergird important personal locations but whose exegetical foundations are eroding. Having said this, Peppiat's reading will probably not solve everything. There are still some issues to be ironed out. But what I would say is that without taking a step in the direction that Peppiatt is traveling, these problems cannot be solved. So it is a highly strategic argument and treatment. I expect it to break the broader discussion open in a new and constructive way.

Douglas Campbell
Professor of New Testament, Duke Divinity School

Acknowledgements

I would first like to thank the scholars who listened to or read a version of my argument, commented on it, and encouraged me to develop it: Ben Blackwell, Douglas Campbell, Nick Crawley, Seth Crawley, Oliver Crisp, Tony Cummins, Lindsey Hall, Brad Jersak, Matt Lynch, Simon Ponsonby, Murray Rae, Alan Spence, Justin Stratis, and David Wenham. In that list are those who both agree and disagree with me, and those who partially agree and partially disagree with me. Everyone pushed me to work out more carefully and more precisely what I was trying to say and how I was trying to say it.

I wish to thank especially my colleagues and friends, Brad Jersak and Matt Lynch. They have read and commented on many versions of my work, and have helped me keep a sense of humor throughout. A highlight of my research was receiving selfies from Matt and Brad sporting their own versions of head coverings. I would also like to thank my editor, Robin Parry, whose interest made this book a reality, and whose edits and questions made it a better book. As always, I am so grateful to my friend and thesis supervisor, Murray Rae. He remains an invaluable conversation partner and critic and continues to push me to improve my work.

My thanks go to my brilliant team and to my trustees at Westminster Theological Centre. They have all been hugely supportive and have encouraged me to make time for research in amongst a busy schedule. I would also like to thank my wonderful little church family who are tolerant of my obsession with Paul and 1 Corinthians, and who teach me what it means to live out cruciform worship.

My special thanks is reserved, as always, for my family. I am forever indebted to my parents, who not only make time to read and comment on my work, but more importantly, who are quite simply the best parents in the world. I am constantly grateful for my four sons, two of whom have become theologians in their own right, and two of whom think like theologians anyway. That they take the time to ask about my work, to listen, to read, and to argue with me is an absolute delight. I particularly wish to thank Seth for his time in editing and formatting my work.

I remain convinced that I would never really achieve anything without my husband, Nick Crawley. I have benefitted more than I can say from his knowledge of Paul's First Letter to the Corinthians, his love of Paul, his insight into Scripture, his prayers, and the hours and hours of his time spent discussing this with me. As with everything I do, this work is partly his.

Introduction

The Backdrop

Reading Paul will never be an easy task. His letters contain challenges for any reader, be they a scholar, lay Christian, or outsider to the Christian faith. The questions surrounding Paul's views on women—particularly in relation to the place women occupy in the church and in worship services—are the source of much controversy. The exegesis of certain passages in Paul touches theological, ecclesial, and pastoral concerns. What is our theology of man and woman? How does this shape our practices in the church? What impact does this have on individuals, relationships, marriages, families, and society? This topic will inevitably evoke strong responses: theological, ecclesial, and pastoral issues are never approached in a detached and objective manner, because too much depends on the outcome. These matters concern how we live our lives together, what our relationships look like, who our leaders and ministers are, and how they behave. These matters take us into questions of authority and power, who exercises power over whom, and how it is implemented. This was not lost on Paul, and these themes emerge in his letters to Corinth. His letters to the Corinthians are directly concerned with issues of authority, power, discernment, wisdom, self-sacrifice, and what it means to be identified with the crucified Christ. Inevitably this includes how men and women behave towards one another, what marriages look like, how the rich treat the poor, and how the church treats those who do not belong. Furthermore, these are not concerns that were only relevant to the first-century church. They are current. In a church where there are often troubled gender relations, what can Paul's letters teach us about how we should treat one another today?

The First Letter to the Corinthians was written in a particular context at a particular time to a particular community addressing their own

1

problems and challenges, mistakes, doctrinal errors, and blind spots. Paul initially spent eighteen months in Corinth evangelizing, teaching, pastoring, discipling, nurturing, and establishing the church. He then left Corinth and set out for Syria with Priscilla and Aquila. Paul arrived in Ephesus where he stayed for a short time and then left, but promised to return to them if God willed. Priscilla and Aquila stayed in Ephesus and Paul went on to Caesarea, Jerusalem, and Antioch (Acts 18:18–22). After ministering to the churches in Asia Minor, Paul then returned to Ephesus, where he stayed for two years. While he was there he began to hear reports about the Corinthian church that caused him some concern and were the occasion of his first letter to the church, which we know about (1 Cor 5:9–11) but which unfortunately no longer exists. Disturbing reports continued to reach Paul from "Chloe's people" informing him of divisions, jealousy, strife, and immorality within the church. Not only this, but he heard of Christians taking their fellow believers to court where "pagans" would pass judgment on spiritual matters instead of the believers resolving them privately in a godly manner. He heard of selfish and ungodly behavior during the Lord's Supper. He became aware of their faulty thinking regarding food sacrificed to idols, sex, marriage, the use of spiritual gifts, the resurrection, and the behavior of women in worship. Three men from Corinth—Stephanas, Fortunatus, and Achaicus—arrived bringing a letter in response to Paul's letter, the response to which is our 1 Corinthians.

The letter is written to admonish the Corinthians for ways in which they have begun to depart from Paul's original teaching and practices, and is a response to their reply to his original epistle. Paul is writing to them regarding certain practices that have become acceptable or normative in his absence, and he is using this letter and his apostolic authority to correct them on certain matters, both theological and pastoral. Their thinking and their practices had drifted away from his original teaching and guidance. Despite assuring the Corinthians that this letter is not written to shame them, but to admonish them as dear children (1 Cor 4:14), it contains many a strong rebuke. For the most part, Paul's corrections are not mild suggestions, but forthright and authoritative directives. First Corinthians does not simply contain the words of a mild-mannered avuncular pastor, but is delivered as a powerful and uncompromising epistle from an apostolic overseer of a young and misguided church, and the Apostle Paul does not pull his punches. Tertullian writes, "the whole first epistle was written . . . not with ink but with gall. It is passionate, indignant, scornful, threatening, harsh; and with respect to each of its various charges, it is directed against certain individuals as chief offenders."¹ Gordon Fee also argues that 1 Corinthians is more than a mild corrective. "[T]he language and style of 1 Corinthians are especially rhetorical and combative. Paul is taking them on at every turn. There is little to suggest that he is either informing or merely correcting; instead, he is attacking and challenging with all the weapons in his literary arsenal."² The force of Paul's argument is significant, as is his perception that his teaching has universal import. Paul informs them that he is planning to send Timothy to remind them of his "ways in Christ as he teaches them everywhere in every church" (1 Cor 4:17), so that they might become imitators of him. Although written in a specific context, we may infer that this teaching is not simply context specific.

This book deals with 1 Corinthians 11–14, and more specifically, three controversial and confusing passages found within these chapters: 11:2–16; 14:20–25; and 14:33b–36. The four aforementioned chapters as a whole are concerned with orderly worship. Two of the passages concern the conduct of women, and one concerns the use of spiritual gifts and the outsider. All these passages contained within this section are marked by what has been variously identified as tensive thought, contradictions, double-mindedness, inconsistencies, and bewildering references throughout. All of them are directed to a congregation that Paul is concerned to correct, and are certainly context-specific, and yet, in most churches, we read the letter to the Corinthians as if it has something to say to *us* today in terms of guiding and shaping *our* lives together. The question of how we read these passages is not simply a dry and academic question. Those who believe that the Bible contains authoritative instruction for Christians in the present are not really at liberty to ignore these passages. They not only touch on the lives of Christians today, but they continue to influence them. The task of interpretation, therefore, is ever with us, and as these passages are still employed as guiding passages for church life and practice, we should be seeking as much clarity as possible.

1. Tertullian, *Treatises on Penance*, 90–91.
2. Fee, *Corinthians*, 5–6.

The Argument: A Summary

In December 2011, I attended a conference at King's College London on Douglas Campbell's work on Romans. I heard arguments for and against his work. Scholars remain divided as to whether Campbell has indeed opened a door to a whole new perspective on Romans; however, his insights into Paul's theology and his research on Paul's use of rhetoric must now be taken into account. Engaging with Campbell's work, I was specifically struck by the possibility that Paul might, at times, use diatribal argumentation in order to make a point, and that he might be doing so more than we realize. Where else might Paul cite his opponents in order to refute them? It is already universally accepted that he quotes some Corinthian slogans in 1 Corinthians in order to make a point. These verses include 6:12, 13; 7:1; 8:1, 8:4; 10:23; and 15:12. It is also recognized that he is responding to a written letter from them (i.e., he is in a "conversation" already). If he had a letter in front of him outlining their thoughts and practices, both of which he wished to correct, might he not have refered to this at greater length in his response? As I explored this possibility in relation to the three passages in chapters 11–14, I began to see a pattern emerging in the text. As I compared 1 Corinthians 11:2–16 with 1 Corinthians 14:33b–36, I found that other scholars have for some time been arguing that Paul was using a rhetorical strategy in the latter passage to argue against the Corinthian men who were trying to silence (possibly married) women. The passage on tongues and prophecy in 14:20–25 is similarly a source of great confusion, containing as it does an apparently inherent contradiction. What if Paul was using a strategy throughout 1 Corinthians 11–14 where he cites his opponents' views from their letter in a more extended fashion in order to refute them, and what if he was doing this more than had previously been acknowledged?

In this book, I argue that Paul is doing precisely that. Although the argument—that Paul is using rhetoric against his opponents—has been proposed by individuals in relation to each of the texts mentioned above, no one has yet explored a possible connection between the three texts, and the possibility that Paul may be using a rhetorical strategy more extensively in this section. That Paul uses rhetoric in his letters is undisputed. That he uses a particular form of rhetoric in these three passages has not yet been generally accepted. I explore the possibility that within 11:2–16, 14:20–25, and 14:33b–36 there are Corinthian ideas, expressions, and theology that have been incorporated and woven into the text among Paul's own ideas, expressions, and theology, and that Paul has done this in such a way as to construct powerful Pauline arguments *against* the Corinthian practices of head coverings for women, speaking in tongues all at once, and banning married women from speaking out in worship services. I demonstrate that reading Paul in this way not only yields coherent arguments within each passage itself, but that these arguments then accord with the letter as a whole, and with the theology found in the wider Pauline corpus. There are, therefore, many reasons, both negative and positive, for exploring a new solution to these passages.

i. The confusion of the texts

The first reason to revisit these texts is the confusion generated, evident both within the texts themselves and in attempts to bring harmony and sense out of them. Within Paul's section on public worship, we find these three passages that mostly confuse, bewilder, and challenge the reader. Making sense of these passages for any reader, scholar or otherwise, is hugely challenging, and they absorb the commentators with their exegetical possibilities and puzzles. They are riddled with inconsistencies, contradictions, and confusing messages and are marked by serious textual and exegetical problems. Yet, despite a plethora of problems with the text, theologians, biblical scholars, and churchmen and women alike continue to hold doggedly to the notion that these verses in their entirety reflect *Paul's* views. The bewildering corollary to this is that those who hold these views begin by admitting their own and everyone else's inability to make sense of the passage under consideration, then go on to outline the astonishing array of interpretations of the terms used within the passage, before finally offering their own interpretation of how it might possibly be read as a coherent whole.

One can find those who attempt to "make sense" of these passages often engaging in elaborate speculation as to the original meanings of words or phrases (sometimes even proposing that Paul uses the same word with two different meanings in sentences that occur one after another). Others give up trying to make sense of Paul and simply state that he must have been confused himself, and still others—in relation to the women passages—just accept (either cheerfully or disgustedly) that Paul was blatantly patriarchal or possibly just a misogynist. In relation to all three passages there is a staggering lack of consensus among scholars as to what Paul might actually have been trying to convey, with New Testament and Pauline experts coming to radically different conclusions from one another. What this book has in common with those who try to bring harmony to these passages is that it attempts to demonstrate that Paul is not only a coherent thinker, but that he is attempting to convey deep spiritual truths in his epistles. Part of what I endeavor to show in this volume is that most attempts to make sense of these passages as examples of Pauline thought in their entirety do, in fact, fail on one count or another. This should spur us on to seek better solutions.

ii. Paul's overall message to the Corinthians

Not only is there internal confusion in the texts, but most of the explanations offered do not agree very easily with Paul's wider thought, both in the letter, and in the Pauline corpus. The first letter to the Corinthians is concerned primarily with addressing disunity among the body, which has been sown by the arrogant, the puffed up, and the immature. Paul enjoins them to make "love" their aim, articulating with great vision and precision what this might look like among them in 1 Corinthians 13, but also throughout the letter. As we have noted, there are many themes in 1 Corinthians: sexual purity, marriage, idolatry, rivalries, secularism, and much more. This volume is concerned with Paul's view on unity in public worship, and how his view of Christlike love is translated into concrete practices within the church. If we begin with the uncontested claim that Paul sees the Lord's Supper as a place where the rich and the well-fed should make way for the poor and marginalized, we begin to see Paul's emphasis here, which runs throughout the letter, that the call to Christlikeness should be lived out by taking the lower part and preferring others. The "higher" the calling in the body of Christ the greater the call to humility, with apostles leading the way down. Paul's own life of apostleship is marked by public shame and dishonor, about which he is clear: apostles are the scum of the earth, a public spectacle. One of the tasks of the exegete is to clarify the role of the passage in the context of the whole epistle. In the light of these observations, we need to be clear, therefore, about what precisely Paul might be saying in chapter 11, for example, if we think that he is now suddenly concerned with establishing or maintaining boundaries based on the glory of men to guard both men and women from "shame" in worship. Similarly, we need to give coherent reasons for why he encourages women to pray and prophesy in public worship while simultaneously telling them to be silent. These are some of the themes that emerge in this book.

Clement, in his First Epistle to the Corinthians, is at great pa.
reiterate the theme of submission, humility, subordination, and the
portance of all members of the body that he sees in Paul's epistle. 1
however, is applied to the entire congregation and not just to the women.
"Even the smallest of our physical members are necessary and valuable to
the whole body; yet all of them work together and also a common subordination, so that the body itself is maintained intact."[3] Moreover, he offers
"shining examples" of both men and women of courage and martyrdom
to inspire the Corinthians to persevere in their faith, and when citing the
story of Rahab, he adds, "Notice, dear friends, how in this woman there was
not only faith, but prophecy also."[4] In the light of these men and women
of faith, "it is a moral duty for us to bow the head and take our seat on the
stool of submission."[5] In addition to the theme of submission and humility
that Clement brings out so clearly, Paul exhorts the Corinthians to take part
in the loving use of spiritual gifts in worship, preferring others, considering
the outsider, and elevating prophecy. We explore the implications of the
overall message of 1 Corinthians in relation to worship for the reading of
our texts.

iii. Paul's wider thought

The third factor in a rereading of these texts includes various aspects of
Paul's wider thought. The first, as Judith Kovacs writes in relation to Paul's
thought, is that "[t]he confession of faith in the crucified and resurrected
Jesus and the hope for his triumphant return have concrete consequences
in the here and now."[6] My premise, therefore, is that Paul's eschatology is
not developed as a longed-for future hope to be realized with the return
of Christ, but that the coming of Christ into the world, and the gift of the
Spirit, has already radically changed human relations in the here and now.
With reference to N. T. Wright's work on *koinonia* in Philemon as an ethical
challenge affecting both slave and free, and Campbell's work on Galatians
3:28, I argue that what can be claimed for the radically new relations of
slave and free, and Jew and Gentile can, *mutatis mutandis*, be claimed for

---

3. Clement, "First Epistle of Clement to the Corinthians," 38.
4. Ibid., 28.
5. Ibid., 49.
6. Kovacs, *1 Corinthians*, xxi.

man and woman.[7] It is quite clear that the phrase ἐν κυρίῳ (in the Lord), which occurs both in Philemon 16 and in 1 Corinthians 11:11, describes and frames a radically new existence. It enables Paul to describe Onesimus as no longer a slave, but now beyond a slave—a beloved brother. If we take seriously the impact of the gospel of Jesus Christ for slave and free, and Jew and Gentile, then what are the implications of the radical new existence for men and women as brothers and sisters "in the Lord" and coheirs with Christ? This must be taken into account when explicating a theology of gender in Paul.

iv. A discernible pattern

One of the most difficult questions for those who wish to argue for a rhetorical reading of Paul is how we can divide up the text when there are no visible cues in terms of quotation marks or markers in the text that we are now "hearing" another voice. Having acknowledged this, there are two key discernible patterns worth noting in 11:2–16, 14:20–25, and 14:33b–36. The first is the obvious "breaks" in the text where we know that there is a shift in thinking, or where Paul appears to be contradicting himself. The second is the use of the rhetorical question. In each example we will note Paul's use of the rhetorical question occurring in 11:13, 14:23, and 14:36. The question that we will be exploring as we look at these passages is this: what answer was Paul expecting by the time he poses these questions to the Corinthians?

v. Where the logic leads . . .

A further problem that this book addresses is the issue of where the logic of these passages leads us if we believe them to be from Paul. I argue that the texts leave us with very little choice as to the thrust of Paul's argument, in that he clearly perceives his correctives to have universal import. Needless to say, for those who do not see the injunctions of Paul as binding on the church today, this will not be a concern. For those who view Scripture as authoritative for contemporary church practice, however, this issue must be faced. First, there is the clear expectation that worship will include the celebration of the Lord's Supper and the gifts of the Spirit, including prophecy

---

7. I refer to Wright, *Paul and the Faithfulness of God*, and Campbell, *The Quest for Paul's Gospel.*

and a circumscribed use of tongues. Second, there is the question of what place women have in public worship. In the course of the book, I highlight some of the more problematic issues for consideration regarding the use of head coverings in church, and the prohibition in chapter 14 against women (or married women) speaking in public worship. If we are hearing the voice of Paul and his emphatic corrections to the church, then we should consider how we might adjust our practices accordingly. Alternative views of the texts are that Paul is simply muddleheaded and inconsistent, holding two different views at once, consequently undermining his own authority. All these views are taken into account.

vi. The historical reconstructions

All interpreters of Paul speculate as to the circumstances to which his letters are addressed. All interpretations of 1 Corinthians depend on a particular set of beliefs regarding the situation in Corinth at the time the letters were written. Some of these beliefs are derived from the text itself. Others are then built around the text in order to paint a picture that makes sense of what we cannot immediately grasp from the text itself. There is no interpretation that does not undergo this process of historical reconstruction. Understanding 1 and 2 Corinthians necessarily entails some form of historical reconstruction, although this is where we find ourselves subject to our own and others' predilections, preconceived ideas about Paul, views on men and women, limited knowledge of Graeco-Roman culture, and a whole host of other subjective and elusive factors.[8] There is no doubt that historical data is very often treated selectively and employed in order to "prove a point," and no work is entirely exempt from this process, my own included. At this stage it should be noted that the process of historical reconstruction is highly problematic. It is, nevertheless, a necessary step in understanding 1 Corinthians. So although we may not shy away from the study of historical data and the process of historical reconstruction, we need to handle historical reconstructions judiciously on the grounds that there is a substantial amount of speculation, prejudice, wish fulfillment, and subjectivity involved in reconstructing the situation in Corinth.[9]

8. See Schüssler Fiorenza, *In Memory of Her*, on the inevitability of the subjective nature of interpretation and historical reconstruction.

9. Holmberg makes the point that we must engage with historical data in our study of Corinthians, even though it is problematic. We cannot divorce the meaning of the text

In the case of 11:2–16 and 14:33b–36, historical reconstructions based on a traditional reading of Paul are universally based on the assumption that there is a problem with the women, rather than a problem with the men. Most commentators take part in the process of "imagining" what might have been the case in Corinth when we attempt to piece together the text in conjunction with what we know of the culture. We are asked to imagine all kinds of scenarios in order to make sense of Paul's thought, but all are predicated on the assumption that it is the women who are rebellious and noncompliant. I question, however, whether it really is easier to imagine a group of wild and rebellious women who are so uncontrollable that they need the intervention of the apostle than it is to imagine the existence of a group of spiritually gifted and highly articulate male teachers who were both overbearing and divisive men. I propose that in a relentlessly patriarchal society, it is more plausible to believe the latter might be the case, that under the men's influential leadership, certain oppressive practices had been implemented, and other destructive and selfish practices had remained unchallenged.

If this is the case then Paul addresses a number of problems in the public worship. The first is that women are being made to veil themselves when praying or prophesying, and being made to do so in a coercive manner. The second is that the self-appointed male leaders are behaving selfishly and greedily at the Lord's Supper. The third is that the Corinthians (or some of them) are exercising spiritual gifts in a way that is unloving and unhelpful, possibly preventing others from taking part in bringing prophetic words, hymns, and revelations to the gathering, acting independently, or ignoring some parts of the body. The fourth is that the "spiritual" tongues-speakers have implemented a strange practice of babbling in tongues all at once on the grounds that they believe this is a powerful witness to unbelievers. The fifth and final problem is that the male leaders are subjecting married women to the requirement of remaining silent.

We know that Paul thought that their meetings were doing more harm than good. The section on worship includes at its heart 1 Corinthians 12:31b—13:13, in which Paul describes the "more excellent way," the way of love which must underpin all Christian worship and life together lest the church become a discordant and harsh noise to those around. The section begins and ends with two passages on the treatment of women in public worship. Traditionally, these have been read as Paul endorsing some sort

---

from its historical context. See "Methods of Historical Reconstruction," 255–71.

of repressive practices in relation to women. I contend, however, that he is saying the *opposite*. If this is true, then what is his point? The community that loves one another as Christ loves, honors women, and gives a voice to the lowest and the least. If we accept a rhetorical reading of these passages it would then mean that Paul begins and ends his section on public worship by addressing the oppression of women, and coming out as strongly as possible *against* it.

A Pauline Church in Corinth?

The questions raised by the three texts in 11–14 must be considered in the context of a wider picture of equality, justice, and caring for the least, highlighted in Paul's censure over their behavior at the Lord's Supper, but permeating his instructions regarding other aspects of public worship. So in addition to preferring the poor at the meal table, *all* (men and women, rich and poor, Jew and Gentile) should be allowed to prophesy, as long as it is done decently and in order; *all* should acknowledge that everyone is needed and appreciated in the body of Christ; all spiritual gifts should be exercised within the primary ethic of love and preference for one another. Paul's rebuke over the unthinking and arrogant use of tongues, and the abuse of the poor and hungry, is consistent with his rebuke over the treatment of women. Tongues had become a divisive weapon, used as a stamp of superior spirituality, rather than a loving gift used to build up the body. Paul warns them that if they speak unintelligible words they will be like foreigners to the ones who hear them (1 Cor 14:11). This defeats the purpose of the Christian community. He is totally uncompromising with the puffed-up Corinthian men who are convinced that they are right on the grounds that they hear from God and are as spiritually gifted as Paul. They are rich, reigning, and boastful, whereas Paul and his companions were a spectacle to men and angels (1 Cor 4:8–13). Paul responds, "If anybody thinks he is a prophet or spiritually gifted, let him acknowledge that what I am writing to you is the Lord's command. If he ignores this, he himself will be ignored" (RSV). Paul pulls his apostolic weight in this matter.

The Scholars' Dismissals

In the following chapters I survey a number of scholars who have considered versions of the argument that Paul employs the rhetorical strategy of citing his opponents in order to refute their views and who have dismissed such an argument. The reasons given for the dismissals are outlined below, but it is not clear that any of these are yet compelling enough to prevent further exploration of this possibility. In the course of the book, I spell out these reasons in more detail, and explain why I do not consider any of them to be decisive enough to prevent the possibility of a rhetorical reading. In brief, the objections can be summarized as follows:

1. Paul is committed to patriarchy and the silencing of women in church so there is no need to posit an alternative reading to 1 Cor 11:2–16 or 1 Cor 14:33b–36.

2. There is nowhere else that Paul cites his opponents using such long passages.

3. There is no signal within the text itself indicating that he might be referring to a Corinthian idea.

There are those who attempt to reconcile the obvious tensions in the text, which I will discuss below, and those who believe that Paul is simply muddleheaded and inconsistent and who thus reject any attempts to "make sense" of him. In response to point 1 above, as many have now pointed out, these passages are strange when weighed against the obvious reality that many of Paul's fellow workers were women. In Romans the names Mary, Tryphaena, Tryphosa, and Persis are mentioned (Rom 16:6, 12). He was happy with women as leaders of house churches (Lydia in Acts 16:14–15 and Phoebe in Rom 16:1). We know of Priscilla and Aquila, who were both leaders and who both discipled Apollos in the faith (Acts 18:26), and Phoebe, who led a church at Cenchreae (Rom 16:1). Paul refers to his friend and coworker Junia as an apostle (Rom 16:7). Furthermore, he is clearly happy with women prophesying and praying in public in Corinth, and obviously approving of Philip's four daughters, who were known as prophets (Acts 21:9). Given the way in which he describes the gift of prophecy as being that which edifies the *whole* church, and given that he elevates the gift of prophecy above the gift of teaching (1 Cor 12:28 is expressed in terms of priority and precedence: *first* apostles, *second* prophets, *third* teachers), it would seem strange for him to implement a contradictory practice that women should stay silent. This poses an immediate problem for the verses on silencing of women.[10]

---

10. Origen responds to the passage in chapter 11 by acknowledging that Paul did allow women to speak, and so defends Paul's later view in chapter 14 by claiming that there

In response to point 2, it is well known that Paul does indeed cite the Corinthians on occasion in his letters. We cannot decide beforehand that he would not do this more extensively if we then find compelling reasons that he might well have done, especially if this also makes better sense of the text.

In response to point 3, this objection is certainly true. We cannot find any signals in the text itself that indicate Paul is about to quote or refer to a Corinthian idea. This, however, is also true of the other verses that scholars have already agreed upon as representing Corinthian slogans, and even appear in quotation marks in our translated text where there is no such punctuation in the original (see for example 1 Cor 6:12 and 10:23 in the RSV). When faced with complex passages, and such a disconcerting array of interpretations, as we will outline, readers should explore all possibilities. Ultimately they will then have to judge for themselves which reading sounds more "convincing" to them.

---

must be a difference in the audience that Paul allows for a woman. In this explanation, he differentiates between "church" and other situations. This position has also been adopted by some contemporary churches where women are permitted to teach other women and children, but not men. However, when articulated here by Origen, this position is clearly seen to be riddled with inconsistencies. That a woman should be recognized as a prophet to the nation, but unable to "speak in church" becomes a little ludicrous. So Origen, "Realising that all were speaking and had permission to speak if a revelation came to them (1 Cor 14:30), Paul says, **The women should keep silence in the churches.** Now the disciples of the women, who had become pupils of Priscilla and Maximilla, not of Christ the bridegroom (see Eph 5:31–32), did not heed this commandment. Let us consider what they say fairly as we reply to their specious arguments. Indeed, let us consider their arguments fairly. They say that there were four daughters of Philip the evangelist, and that they prophesied (Acts 21:9). 'And,' they assert, 'if these women prophesied, why is it not appropriate for our prophetesses to prophesy?' Our response is as follows: First, if you say 'our women prophesied,' show us the signs of prophecy in them. Second, even if the daughters of Philip prophesied, they did not speak in the churches—we do not find this reported in the Acts of the Apostles. Nor is this found in the Old Testament. Yes, it is attested that Deborah was a prophetess, and *Miriam the sister of Aaron, taking a drum, led off the women* (Exod 15:20). But you will not find it written that Deborah publicly addressed the people, as Jeremiah and Isaiah did. Nor will you find that Huldah, who was a prophetess, spoke to the people, but only to a one person who came to her (2 Kings 22:14–20). 'But,' they will say, 'the Gospel also mentioned *Anna a prophetess, the daughter of Phanuel, of the tribe of Asher*' (Luke 2:36). Yes, but she did not speak in the church. Therefore, even if we should concede, on the basis of a prophetic sign, that a woman is prophetess, still she is **not permitted to speak** in church. When Miriam the prophetess spoke, it was to certain women whom she was leading. **For it is shameful for a woman to speak in church.** *And I permit no woman to teach or to have authority over men* (1 Tim 2:12)." Kovacs, *1 Corinthians*, 239–40.

A Rhetorical Pattern

Part of the process of discernment must be to consider all the options before us. For this reason, I devote considerable attention to traditional interpretations of these passages, all based on the idea that the entire passage reflects Paul's views. I consider each passage in turn, but reserve the majority of comment for 1 Corinthians 11:2–16 on the grounds that this is a longer and more complex passage than the other two, and that if we can make a convincing argument for a rhetorical reading of 11:2–16, then a similar pattern in the other two passages becomes more obvious. Beginning with 1 Corinthians 11, therefore, I propose that Paul is interlacing different strands of thought and various assertions: his teaching, the Corinthians' mistaken construal of his teaching and their own claims based on a blend of Paul's teaching and their own theology, an exposure of the absurdity and aggression of their practices, and his own response, ending with an apostolic threat should they defy his rulings.[11] Elements of this strategy can then be seen more clearly in 1 Corinthians 14: 33b–36 and 14: 20–25.

As we have noted, a mark of all these passages is the ability to confuse the reader. They are often described as being "double-minded." What if an explanation for this is that there are indeed two "minds" at work? As we have noted, the Corinthians knew the other "half of the conversation."[12] Either they had supplied it in their letter in the form of the very words that Paul cites back to them, or he is referring to situations that they all know very well. We are coming in at what John Coolidge Hurd has labelled "stage 3" of the process: Paul has written to them, they have written back,

---

11. The idea that Paul's vocabulary and expression is complex because he would have been using the vocabulary and expression of his hearers as well as his own has been explored by Terence Paige. Paige makes the point in relation to Paul's use of Stoic vocabulary and thought, which we will refer to in due course. Here, however, I wish to note Paige's point about Paul using the language of his hearers for the sake of effective communication. He writes, "The question I wish to raise is *not* whether or not *Paul* thought in Stoic manner; rather, could it be that he is writing to people who themselves use such language, think in a Stoicizing manner, or are impressed with Stoic ideas? Otherwise why does he so frequently use language that appears Stoic, though he operates with different assumptions? After all, the manner of Paul's expression is not shaped solely by his Jewish background and Christian confession, but surely to some extent by the needs of his audience as well? Do not their problems, vocabulary, and level of understanding influence the manner of the apostle's communication with them?" "Stoicism, ἐλευθερία and Community at Corinth," 209.

12. Richards, *Paul and First-Century Letter Writing*, 15.

and this is Paul's response.[13] It is entirely plausible that there are two voices woven into the text: the Corinthians' voice and Paul's voice. It is also entirely plausible that it is not a case of a simple dissection of the passage into "Paul" and the "Corinthians" on the grounds that they are in the middle of a dialogue. It is more likely, given that Paul lived with them and taught them for eighteen months, that the expressions and thoughts of each party has been influenced by the other. However, if it is possible from the clues in the text to identify whose voice is whose in the letter, and in Paul's overall theology, then it can be demonstrated that Paul is indeed arguing *against* and not *for* certain practices in these passages. I contend that it is precisely that feature which we find confusing and baffling about the texts—namely, their incoherence—that is the clue to understanding them.

A Constellation of Ideas

In 1 Corinthians we are faced with a complex interplay of ideas that has arisen as a result of a relationship between Paul and the church(es) that has been going on for a number of years. The Corinthians have been deeply influenced by Paul's teaching, his ideas, and his personality, but like all Christians, their thinking continues to be influenced by the surrounding culture. The constellation of ideas and practices that Paul confronts, therefore, is likely to be a blend of his own teaching, somewhat corrupted perhaps, ideas from the surrounding culture, and the thinking of the fledgling Christian community itself. It is no wonder that we struggle to extricate "his" ideas from "theirs." They are interwoven. Like all heresies and misinterpretations of orthodox teaching, there are subtle elements of the "right" teaching embedded in the "wrong" teaching, because that is what the wrong teaching is based on in the first place.

This epistle was carefully crafted and written by Paul, but as a response to previously written letters both by him and the Corinthians. It is addressed to people he knows and is already communicating with. They have held to some but not all of his teaching. They have come under other influences. There have been various studies of 1 Corinthians arguing that the Corinthians were particularly influenced by one specific philosophy or school of thought over and above others, be it Epicureanism, Cynicism, Stoicism, Gnosticism, Hellenistic Judaism, or secularism.[14] Instead of mak-

13. See Hurd, *The Origin of 1 Corinthians*.

14. See Adams and Horrell, "Scholarly Quest for Paul's Church at Corinth," 1–43, for

ing a case here for one particular dominant school of thought behind their ideas, I am suggesting that there are a multitude of influences that have been brought to bear on the Corinthians, one of them Paul's own teaching, and that he and they share phrases and ideas, but have come to use them and apply them in different ways.

The Voice(s) of Paul

The first chapter examines a summary of some of the traditional readings of 11:2–16, noting the labyrinthine nature of scholarly comment on this text, as well as highlighting some of the inconsistencies between the many readings and within the readings themselves. The numerous problems that we find should in themselves cause us to pause before claiming that one or the other of these readings is the "definitive" reading. In the second chapter I explore 1 Corinthians 11:7–16 in more detail, examining the implications that these verses have for a theology of men and women if we take seriously the proposal that these verses reflect Paul's views. In the third and fourth chapters I offer an alternative reading of the text, identifying where I believe Paul is referring to his own ideas, and then to a Corinthian idea, or previously written phrase, or practice, through which he is challenging them to abandon the practice of head coverings as there is "no such custom" in any other church. I include a brief summary of how 1 Corinthians 14:33b–36 aligns with a rhetorical reading of chapter 11. The fifth chapter focuses on the tongues and prophecy passage in 14:20–25, noting similar patterns. The final chapter explores some of the implications for church life and worship if we were to accept a rhetorical reading. Lastly, I have included an appendix indicating where I believe Paul is alluding to a Corinthian idea, phrase, or claim, and where he is speaking with his own voice.

Having established that the entire question of "evidence" is slippery, I will nevertheless offer my own contextual and theological evidence for this reconstruction, as well as demonstrating how it brings a logic to the passages themselves. With regard to textual and linguistic evidence, we will also explore where there are clues for a rhetorical reading. This book does not include a close exploration of any attempt to identify specifically Pauline and/or non-Pauline words or phrases within the text, or an attempt to demonstrate from the grammar or structure of the text where we might be able to identify a non-Pauline voice. It is not my intention to claim that

a brief summary of the history of scholarship.

a rhetorical reading can be "proven" in this way. It may be that some sort of close textual work aimed at separating Pauline and non-Pauline words could be pressed into service in relation to this argument, but close textual work abounds, with predictably varied results, and this is not the goal of this book.[15] Instead, this is written in order to demonstrate the fragility and inconsistencies of the existing interpretations of these three passages while at the same time offering a solution that, although not yet perfect, contains more than enough internal consistency to warrant a hearing, while at the same time harmonizing with the letter as a whole, as well as reflecting Paul's wider theology and practice.

Paul and Women

In recent years it has become more and more commonplace for theologians and biblical scholars to be candid about their own particular bias or background when approaching a theological topic or a biblical text. It is part of a general recognition that there is no "neutral" or objective reading, as well as contributing to a desire for transparency, that one declares her "colors" from the outset. Autobiographical detail is never insignificant in our reading of any text, and the Bible is no exception. Paul is a highly controversial figure, and his writings so often elicit a strong response. One of the premises underlying this book is that Paul is a brilliant theologian, a man of extraordinary insight, and a careful, deliberate, and scholarly man of God. This is not always people's view of Paul: he speaks differently to different people.

My own journey towards the great respect that I hold for Paul as a man and a theologian began when I was twenty-four years old. For most of my adult life, I have been part of the evangelical charismatic church, but before that I really had very little to do with the evangelical church, apart from perhaps adopting something of an antagonistic stance. Consequently, I was sheltered from many of the controversies that plague evangelical men and women, and it was only in later life, when I began to study theology, that I discovered what a highly controversial figure Paul was and is, and what emotions he evokes in those outside and inside the church. My recollection is that I was brought up on stories about Jesus, and some of the

15. For the most detailed account of this passage as an interpolation, see Walker, *Interpolations in the Pauline Letters*. Walker argues that the passage is composed of three separate texts, the whole section is an interpolation, and that none of these texts is from Paul.

Old Testament stories and Psalms, but I was never "taught" Paul in Sunday school or church and so in some ways I came to him blissfully ignorant. When I did read the Bible for the first time properly I was an adult and I read it cover to cover. This meant that after the Old Testament, the Gospels came first, followed by Acts, followed by Paul's epistles. As a consequence, I read Paul through Jesus. Encountering Jesus in the Gospels, I was struck by his love for women and was drawn to it. I was certainly baffled by certain passages in Paul, but I think at that stage I just glossed over them. These strangely negative passages about women seemed to be outweighed in my mind first by the teachings and behavior of Jesus, and then by other passages in Paul's letters where I saw his passion for mutual respect, forgiveness, and self-sacrificing love between all peoples, including men and women. I recognized that he worked with women, that he expected them to serve in every aspect of church life, and that he sometimes referred to his own experience in feminine terms. I liked him, and over the years, I came to love his writings. Consequently, I am a sympathetic reader of Paul. Against the usual feminist reading of Paul, therefore, I assumed from the outset that as a man who had known Jesus Christ, he was not against women, but indeed, must have been "on our side."[16] This has been one significant aspect of my approach to Paul.

The second significant experiential factor was that in my journey towards God and into the church, I had encountered the power and gifts of the Holy Spirit. I was struck by how—both in Scripture and in the church life of my experience—the Spirit is poured out on, and pours out gifts on, men and women alike. In practice, there is no gender discrimination in the apportioning of the Spirit's gifts, so why would there be any division of labor in terms of what is expected of us in God's kingdom? A pneumatological understanding of calling and vocation leads to an uncompromisingly equitable structure. What disturbed me, however, was that I became more and more aware of the teaching on Paul in evangelical denominations and I realized what a powerful weapon the Bible could be against the participation of women in ministry, and how damaging this has been and is for both men and women inside and outside of the church.

16. For feminist readings of Paul where Paul is understood to be attempting to silence the women, see MacDonald, *The Pauline Churches*, and Wire, *The Corinthian Women Prophets*.

Having personally glossed over the difficult passages regarding women for many years, I found the topic of Paul and men and women became a subject that I was less and less able to ignore.

Gordon Fee's work on Paul and the Spirit was an inspiration to me. With Fee's careful and sympathetic exposition coupled with my own experiences, I saw Paul's emphasis on the work of the Spirit in all his writings, as well as what I believed was his commitment to women in leadership in the church. This view, however, is in stark contrast to those who believe Paul was committed to the subordination of women to men, or to either an exclusively or even an ultimately male leadership in the church. As a result, I also believed that as a church we needed to continue to wrestle with the texts that have been used to prevent women from participating in all ministries and forms of service.

Thus, we have a number of choices when faced with Paul's passages on women. Furthermore, the choices that we have already made regarding the Bible, Paul, and how the biblical voices speak to men and women will color the way we read. There is no escaping this. It may be that you, the reader of Paul, are already convinced that he (a) is committed to patriarchy, (b) is a hopeless and offensive misogynist, (c) holds different views in tension, (d) is confused and oscillates in his thinking, or (e) ruled on certain practices regarding women that were only appropriate to his day and therefore not binding upon us today. This book explores a sixth perspective: that Paul understood that women enjoy a new status in Christ that liberates them, both in terms of their identity in relation to Christ and also in relation to men, and that an appreciation of this new identity led to him implementing practices in the church that allowed women to participate equally in all forms of ministry and service. Not only this, but that Paul believed these views should be reflected within the entire body of Christ.

This book is not only about Paul and women, but also about Paul and his views on the ethics of public Christian worship and how it affects all the participants. This cannot help but shed light on his views on women, but is also linked to his general concern for those of low status in his society.

There are two reasons that I have chosen to focus on a third passage in chapters 11–14, a passage on the use of tongues and prophecy in public worship. The first is that the structure of the passage is very similar to the passages on women in chapters 11 and 14 and thus we can see a pattern emerging in all three. The second reason is that the content of the passage, when read as a refutation of Corinthian ideas and practices, sheds even greater light on Paul's general rebuke for the Corinthian church, and why he felt the need to intervene. In other words, what is going on between the Corinthians and Paul in the tongues passage is all part of a bigger picture and contributes to how we might understand the overall picture of what he was targeting and why.

1 Corinthians 11:2–16

The Problems with the Women

Introduction

First Corinthians 11:2–16 is notorious for being one of the most problematic texts in the New Testament. Not only has it been the subject of numerous commentaries and endless debate among scholars, but it has also caused bewilderment and disagreement among churchgoing Christians. Some have wondered how they should respond to the fact that Paul appears to be saying that all women in church should be wearing head coverings. Certain denominations have simply understood this passage to mean that women should *definitely* be wearing some form of head covering in church (shawls, hats, drapes).[1] Still others attempt to explain this passage away on the grounds that it only has cultural relevance to the time of Paul, and is therefore not binding on the church today. Finally, it is probably fair to say that the majority of Christians simply ignore it. The reasons for these diverse reactions are rooted in the text itself. It is certainly not straightforward and thus gives rise to a diversity of interpretation and response.

As has often been observed, the exegetical problems associated with interpreting 1 Corinthians 11:2–16 are numerous. Philip Payne notes, with reference to commentators of the recent past, the following: "C. F. D. Moule writes that the problems raised by 1 Corinthians 11:2–16 'still await a really

---

1. Someone told me of a young woman who sat in the front of church with an orange mixing bowl on her head in protest to being made to "cover her head." Apparently no one said a word. I also heard of a young woman who stood up to bring a prophetic word only to find a dirty tea towel being thrown over her head by an obliging older woman as there was nothing else at hand.

convincing explanation.' G. B. Caird writes, 'It can hardly be said that the passage has yet surrendered its secret,'" and "W. Meeks regarded it as one of the most obscure passages in the Pauline letters."[2] More recent commentators do not particularly claim to be any the wiser. Craig Blomberg's view is that "[t]his passage is probably the most complex, controversial, and opaque of any text of comparable length in the New Testament. A survey of the history of interpretation reveals how many different exegetical options there are for a myriad of questions and should inspire a fair measure of tentativeness on the part of the interpreter."[3]

Fee states the matter thus:

> Along with these larger contextual questions, this passage is full of notorious exegetical difficulties, including (1) the "logic" of the argument as a whole, which in turn is related to (2) our uncertainty about the meaning of some absolutely crucial terms and (3) our uncertainty about prevailing customs, both in the culture(s) in general and in the church(es) in particular (including the whole complex question of early Christian worship). Thus the two crucial contextual questions, what was going on and why, are especially difficult to reconstruct.[4]

First, Fee identifies the three basic problems with the passage: the logic of the passage, our uncertainty about the crucial terms, and our uncertainty about prevailing customs, both in society and in early Christian worship. This, he posits, leaves us with numerous problems when trying to reconstruct the situation at Corinth, the contents of Paul's previous letter, or possibly letters, and the Corinthians' response to this earlier correspondence. In addition to this, Fee notes that there is considerable "uncertainty" about "some absolutely crucial terms," and notes in particular the exegetical difficulties surrounding the terms: "head," "having down the head," "uncovered," "glory," "authority over her head," "because of the angels," "in the place of a shawl," and "such a custom."[5] These, it turns out, are in fact nearly *all* the crucial terms in the passage. We may add as well the terms for "man" and "woman." Not only is there a lack of consensus among scholars as to what these terms mean, but the debates are heated, and those arguing for

2. Moule, *Worship in the New Testament*, 65; Caird, "Paul and Women's Liberty," 278; Meeks, *The Writings of St. Paul*, 38, cited in Payne, "Wild Hair," 9.

3. Blomberg, *NIV Application Commentary*, 214.

4. Fee, *Corinthians*, 492.

5. Ibid., 492.

a particular reading, quite naturally, argue that theirs must be correct. Any lay person wishing to understand this passage will find himself or herself completely rudderless in a sea of erudite biblical and historical scholarship, having no real means of adjudicating between the arguments presented, and with an overriding impression that this passage is both obscure and confusing.

In this chapter, we will explore a number of approaches to 1 Corinthians 11:2-16 in which the commentators attempt to bring out a coherence to Paul's argument in these verses. The scholars that we examine in this chapter can be characterized as having a reasonably moderate and accommodating approach to Paul and are united in their attempts to give him the benefit of the doubt when it comes to both his views and his argument, advocating that it is possible to read this text without taking offense either at Paul's view of women, or his ability to construct a coherent argument. We will begin by examining their general argument, noting both the strengths and weaknesses and the diversity of approach regarding some of the contested terms in the passage. In exploring a variety of approaches we will highlight the difficulties within the text itself as well as the challenge of adjudicating between the different arguments as to what the Greek text actually means. We will conclude by pressing these arguments to their logical conclusions in relation to the behavior of the women of Corinth.

Head Coverings or Hairstyles?

Traditional readings of this passage understand the whole passage as reflecting the opinions and theology of Paul himself, and these readings could be seen to fall broadly into four categories. There is first of all a major disagreement as to whether Paul is speaking of head coverings or hairstyles/ hair length (I will use hairstyle to refer to both hair style and length). The first two categories, therefore, can be divided into either a "head coverings" reading or a "hairstyle" reading. The second sharp disagreement is over whether Paul is ultimately arguing for a patriarchal and subordinationist view of God, creation, men and women, or whether, in fact, he redefines and thus undermines (his own) hierarchical views in the end. Readings of 1 Corinthians 11:2-16 could be categorized as (a) head coverings/hierarchical, (b) head coverings/nonhierarchical, (c) hairstyle/hierarchical, and (d) hairstyle/nonhierarchical. As hierarchical and patriarchal views of the relation of women to men are becoming more and more embarrassing for the church, there are a number of contemporary scholars who argue that Paul holds two views "in tension." In other words, it is argued that he is both patriarchal and egalitarian, thus apparently letting Paul off the hook when it comes to teaching practices that smack of gross inequality or misogyny. However, most of these commentators end up arguing that Paul *also* holds to a soft patriarchy as an overarching view, which is, in essence, hierarchical. So, although the commentators themselves argue that they can read Paul in a way that demonstrates that he is nonhierarchical or even "egalitarian,"[6] I will argue that in reality, if we hold to a traditional reading of Paul, we are left only with either head coverings/hierarchical or hairstyles/hierarchical. I will give examples of all these readings in due course, demonstrate how confusing and muddled the issues become when we follow certain arguments through, and suggest that we cannot avoid drawing certain conclusions about Paul and his view of the nature and status of men and women before God if we take the traditional view.

Questions to note as we explore the range of explanations for Paul's thought are: Is this about head coverings or hairstyles? Why does Paul want men to pray and prophesy with their heads uncovered? Why does he want women to pray and prophesy with their heads covered? Who is this shaming and why? What is the relationship of cultural practice to theological principle? What does he see as the relationship of man to woman, woman to man, man to Christ, woman to Christ, Christ to God, etc.? What is the theology of glory that he is expressing? Does Paul really believe that attire carries *theological* significance in relation to gender roles and also to God? Who are the angels and why do they matter? Why does he appear to contradict himself? Why does he refer to praying and prophesying in verse 5 and just praying in verse 13? Why is Paul so adamant about this? Further to these questions, we must also ask, if this is Paul and if we read him aright,

6. I use the word "egalitarian" in relation to others' arguments to describe a view of Paul's position only because it is a word that is understood to mean a belief that men and women are (a) created equally and (b) equally able to participate in all areas of ministry and service in the church. To use it thus, however, only in relation to gender is, I believe, an aberrative use of the word. All Christians should be "egalitarians" without question on the basis that Christians believe all human beings are equally made "in the image of God," all are equally "sinners," and those who are saved are all equally saved. Similarly, to use "egalitarian" in opposition to "complementarian" is to employ two misnomers at once. "Complementarians" would more accurately be designated subordinationists, while most "egalitarians" could happily co-opt the term "complementarian," on the basis that male and female are deemed to complement one another in their difference in mutual and reciprocal relations.

and if we can identify the practices that he is instituting and enforcing, why do those who believe that the Bible is authoritative, or at least normative, for church life and practice not adhere to these practices today?

The Traditional Readings

i. The centrality of shame and honor

The passage in question falls in a section where Paul is discussing propriety in public worship, including the use of spiritual gifts, the celebration of the Lord's Supper, and two discussions on the behavior of women, which bracket this section (chs. 11–14). As we have noted, there are two main versions of the traditional view: one arguing that Paul is ruling that women (either all women or married women) should wear head coverings, while simultaneously ruling that men should not, and a second view that Paul is saying that women should wear their hair long, but bound up, while men should wear their hair short. Both arguments are predicated on the notion that Paul is making such a ruling to guard both men and women from shame and dishonor in the eyes of God, one another, and the angels. This is seen to be in keeping with the theme of propriety in worship—what is acceptable and what is *seen* to be acceptable in public—and is based on Paul's opening claims in verses 4–5, "Any man who prays or prophesies with something on his head disgraces his head, but any woman who prays or prophesies with her head unveiled disgraces her head—it is one and the same thing as having her head shaved." There have been a number of versions of this argument put forward by scholars. I will outline just a few, but note that there are countless scholars who offer a version of the shame/honor argument, often with very slight variations. The substance is the same; Paul is concerned with how things appear, and that shame and honor between sexes is both reflected in and symbolized by outward appearance or attire (hairstyle or head covering). This argument, though apparently simple in its content, is extraordinarily complex in its logic. In what follows we will explore a range of attempts to explicate the "logic" of the passage.

ii. Shame/honor and head coverings

Anthony Thiselton, in his shorter commentary on 1 Corinthians, argues that when Paul refers to head coverings for women, he is indeed referring to a "common apostolic tradition." Thiselton reads this passage as directed to both men and women in the Corinthian church, "warning them not to veer off into self-styled practices."[7] With respect to the women, Thiselton suggests that there may have been some who "wanted to break free from more conventional roles or constraints on the basis of gospel 'freedom' and gender equality." In his view, "[t]o throw off gender restraints on the grounds that both genders were equally free seemed legitimate from the viewpoint of women who had leadership qualities."[8] He even adds that "[a]pparently Paul approved of their new freedom to lead in prayer, to utter prophetic speech, or to preach longer 'prophetic' reflections in public worship. Such women understandably no longer wished to be categorized as 'modest violets' among the more forceful married women of Roman society. So they showed off their 'freedom' publicly."[9] However, rather than wondering why Paul would not also approve of these women being free of the need for a head covering in order to prophesy or pray in public, on the grounds that they are indeed "free" in Christ, Thiselton posits that Paul was most concerned at this stage about etiquette and how things appear. Paul, says Thiselton, "believes that this [practice] is shaming them and others around them." Here then, Paul is speaking about respect for the "other."

On the question of whether Paul is addressing all men and women or only married men and women, Thiselton appears to make a slightly different point in his later, shorter commentary than he does in the earlier commentary. In the earlier work he points out that the NRSV chooses "husband" in verse 3 to translate ὁ ἀνήρ instead of "man"—where the REB, NJB, and NIV all choose "man"—and writes, "[a] few commentators defend *husband*, but the overwhelming majority of writers convincingly argue that the issue concerns gender relations as a whole, not simply those within the more restricted family circle."[10] It appears here that Thiselton believes that the weight of opinion is on "man" and "woman" rather than husbands and wives. If Paul is addressing only married men and women, rather than expecting *all* women to be covered in front of *all* men, then this provides a different rationale for Paul's views on head coverings, but this does not appear to have widespread support. As he also notes, it might be argued

---

7. Thiselton, *First Corinthians*, 171.

8. Ibid., 173.

9. Ibid.

10. Thiselton, *The First Epistle*, 822.

that Paul is addressing the question of women in relation to a significant familial man (husband, uncle, father), but again this is difficult to prove.

In his later commentary, however, Thiselton places more emphasis on the behavior of married women in relation to a husband and married men in relation to a wife, but at the same time also refers to more general practices of respectful attire of all men and all women. Despite using the terms "man" and "woman" to translate the Greek terms, he appears to be saying that Paul is referring to a "hood" or veil, which is the mark of a respectable married woman in Roman society,[11] and implies that Paul is actually addressing married women in this passage. With reference to verse 5 he writes: "With evenhandedness Paul now turns to the (married) **woman**. It is beyond doubt that in Roman society a hood (or perhaps a *veil*) was what a married woman was expected to wear *in public* as a mark of *respectability*." Without this veil, a married woman was inviting men to "size her up."[12] In addition to this, Thiselton argues that Paul is evenhanded in his treatment of men and women, claiming a complete reciprocity and mutuality in Paul's treatment of both. His emphasis, however, is again on husbands and wives. With respect to the men, Thiselton claims neither a head covering nor long hair would be appropriate in front of a man's *wife*, as both would be demeaning in some way. "What is worn or not worn serves as a mark of *respect to one's husband or wife*."[13] His point, therefore, is that regardless of the translation (man/husband, woman/wife), Paul's concern is primarily to do with signs of respect between the sexes, but in his explanation of what is happening in the Corinthian church, the emphasis is certainly on what was expected in the culture of the time for married men and women. Thiselton does not refer here to any creation ordinances as possible reasons for the wearing or not of head coverings. We will come to this question in due course.

Thiselton concludes that Paul is saying: "Do you want the church to appear as those who have no respect at all for norms that invite respect in society at large? It is one thing for a woman to share with men in the ministry of prayer and preaching. It is quite another thing to substitute 'sameness' for mutuality, reciprocity, and an ethos for respect and respectability."[14] The two problems then are associated with (1) a throwing off of gender

11. Thiselton, *First Corinthians*, 170.
12. Ibid., 173.
13. Ibid., 172.
14. Ibid., 177.

restraints and (2) a lack of respect. We will return below to the question of what is demeaning or not for either sex, and why. For now, it is clear that Thiselton's main argument in his later commentary rests on notions of respect for the other sex, including specifically within marriage, and that his argument rests on the question of cultural norms. Despite noting in his earlier commentary the problems with translating "man" and "woman" as "husband" and "wife," he proposes in his later commentary that Paul's primary goal is to safeguard honor between the married men and women. Moreover, he attempts within his argument to credit Paul with some kind of egalitarian perspective through arguing that both sexes are expected to respect one another in an equal fashion. The women must wear clothing that conveys modesty and sexual purity, and refrain from behaving in a provocative manner. The men must not cover their heads or grow their hair long.

Fee's argument centers around similar themes, and displays the same tension between wishing to affirm Paul's commitment to the freedom of the Christian man and woman from outward expressions of piety and his respect for the customs of the day. He acknowledges that the gospel Paul preached would have given newfound freedom to the women in his churches, but also believes this freedom to be the very cause of their temptation to push the boundaries. No one can deny that Paul allowed women to participate in worship by praying and prophesying. The underlying premise in both Fee's and Thiselton's arguments is that, sadly, Paul's leniency towards the women appears to have been abused. He gave them an inch, and they took a mile. Like Thiselton, Fee is at great pains to argue for a more egalitarian reading of 1 Corinthians 11:2–16. Both scholars are adamant that a head covering for a woman is not a sign of a woman's inferiority or subordination, but that it is simply a mark of respect, both for the woman herself, and for the man/husband. Fee also argues against the idea that a man would have any authority over a woman, on the grounds that "head" should be translated as "source" or "origin" rather than "authority." We will return to the meaning of "head" in a later section. Should the veil then be understood as a sign of the woman's *own* authority rather than a sign that a man has authority over her? This is certainly another alternative reading. Again, we will explore a number of interpretations of this verse below. Like Thiselton, however, Fee contends that the Corinthian women were practicing a custom they believed they were entitled to in their newfound freedom, but which Paul himself disapproved of.[15] "As a part of their new 'spirituality' they were disregarding some very customary distinctions between the sexes that would otherwise have been regarded as disgraceful."[16] This passage is to be understood, therefore, in the context of Paul's concern that all should be done "decently and in order." Fee's and Thiselton's readings would be categorized as head coverings/nonhierarchical.

iii. Shame/honor and partial patriarchy

Commentators like Thiselton, Judith Gundry-Volf, and Alan Johnson attempt to view the passage as a whole, claiming that there are ways of reconciling Paul's thought around common themes. Thiselton identifies unifying themes such as "self-discipline, restraint, and respect for 'the other,' already prominent in 8:1—11:1."[17] Gundry-Volf seeks a different solution, claiming that we cannot reduce Paul's thought *either* to a hierarchical *or* an egalitarian framework as neither does justice to the complexity of the theological issue for Paul. She fully acknowledges the tension in Paul's thought between a hierarchical and patriarchal view of men and women on the one hand and a mutual and reciprocal view on the other, signaled by the break in verse 11, but argues that the solution is not to prioritize one over the other, but to continue to hold the two views in tension under the complexity of Paul's theological *method*. This, she notes, is "characterized by the interplay of culture, creation, and eschatological life in Christ as mutually interpretive loci of theological reflection."[18] So she explores ways of accounting for the tension in Paul's thought as, in her view, ruling in favor of one over the other is "reductionistic."[19] Paul's theological method, in response to his context, becomes the unifying feature of his argument.

According to Gundry-Volf, Paul sets up a gender-distinctive and patriarchal creation order which must then be held in conjunction with a gospel order of reciprocity and mutuality. Paul has a "complex view of creation" and "can read creation within a patriarchal framework as well as an

15. Fee, *Corinthians*, 498.

16. Ibid.

17. See Gundry-Volf, "Gender and Creation," 151–71; Johnson, *1 Corinthians*; Thiselton, *The First Epistle,* 803.

18. Gundry-Volf, "Gender and Creation," 152.

19. Ibid., 165.

egalitarian one," at one and the same time.[20] So, on the one hand, Paul can "appeal to creation to support instructions which presume a hierarchical relationship of man and woman as well as undergird their new social equality in Christ without denying their difference."[21] Gundry-Volf's rationale for these two "contrasting" readings of creation are that they are rooted in two contrasting social contexts: on the one hand, the hierarchically structured shame/honor society, on the other, the "cultic context of Corinthian worship that burst the patriarchal framework."[22] So where Paul had encouraged pneumatic corporate worship where men and women prayed and prophesied equally, he also required the congregation to exercise caution in public worship in order that their social acceptability would not be "diminished" or their "missionary task hindered."[23] Gundry-Volf fully acknowledges the contrast between Paul's views in 11:7–9 and 11:11–12. She does not, however, acknowledge that this contrast might be so marked as to undermine either view. It is acceptable, in her view, that Paul would use Genesis 2 to establish the "priority" of man over woman in the light of the fact that he is the image and glory of God,[24] while at the same time demonstrating that "in the Lord" the "inequality through gender-based priority is removed."[25] The Corinthians simply have to wear two "hats" at once: one where men and women pray and prophesy equally and one in response to the Corinthian setting where the shame/honor paradigm reigns.[26]

There are a number of difficulties here. One occurs in the relation of Paul's appeal to creation noted by Gundry-Volf and the use of this, apparently, to persuade the Corinthians not to practice anything that will cause *social* shame. We will discuss this apparent connection below, but for now note that for many exegetes this remains unproblematic. Johnson is persuaded by this argument, agreeing that Gundry-Volf "makes a careful exegetical case that Paul's chief concern was to correct a practice in Corinthian worship that incurred serious social shame not only on certain male and female individuals but on the church as a whole." For Johnson, this "shame-producing activity involved boundary-transgressing hairstyles that blurred

20. Ibid.,152.
21. Ibid.
22. Ibid.
23. Ibid., 154–55.
24. Ibid., 165.
25. Ibid., 163.
26. Ibid., 168.

gender distinctions between males and females during worship."[27] Johnson is right to infer that Gundry-Volf interprets the problem to have manifested itself in inappropriate hairstyles, although somewhat confusingly, Gundry-Volf continues to refer to "head-coverings" (admittedly sometimes when citing others, but at times in her own words) and even uses the term "head-dress" on occasion, leaving the reader unsure of where the problem, and therefore the solution, actually lies.[28]

The second difficulty is the blurring of the concepts of "difference" and "hierarchy" in relation to male and female. Whereas it is quite clear to me how one could argue that Paul views men and women as different and equal (which is how I would describe his views), it is less clear how one can argue that Paul views men and women *at one and the same time* as being in a hierarchical relationship of superiority and inferiority or pre-eminence and derivation (rooted in creation theology) *and* equal in status (also rooted in creation theology as well as their new status "in the Lord"). So Johnson, on the one hand, argues that Paul desires gender *distinctions,* but what he means by that is that he believes Paul is supportive of practices that signify the subordination of women to men in worship, supports aspects of gender hierarchy, and accepts "the shame-honor pattern, including women's inferiority, as assumed in Mediterranean cultures of the first century." On the other hand, he goes on, "in contrast to this reading, he gives also a fully egalitarian, redemptive reading of creation where male and female are mutually and equally dependent on one another."[29] Johnson and Gundry-Volf both admit to a "contrast" and "tension," but Johnson goes on to admit that this is "an uneasy tension" rather than a wholly reconcilable one.[30] Johnson writes, against Murphy-O'Connor, Thiselton, Hooker, and Fitzmyer, that Paul is not concerned here with sexual immodesty (or homosexuality, which we will come to in due course), nor does he believe that Paul's argument is directed towards the excesses of the women's liberation movement.[31] In agreement with Gundry-Volf, he contends that Paul's

27. Johnson, *1 Corinthians*, 181.

28. In a footnote, Gundry-Volf writes that it is probably best to assume that "covering the head here refers to hairstyles, since in the first-century Roman context there was no social shame associated with women's not veiling or with men's wearing a *himation* over the head . . ." "Gender and Creation," 151 fn.1. She then goes on to discuss the problem with reference to head coverings, headdress, and hairstyles.

29. Johnson, *1 Corinthians*, 182.

30. Ibid., 184–85.

31. Ibid., 193.

"explicit purpose is to avoid causing shame and correspondingly that each bring honor to their head."[32] On the question of the "glory" of man, and also here in agreement with Gundry-Volf, Johnson states "in the cultural social order the woman 'owed' honor to the man because she was the 'glory' of the man by creation."[33] She is created from man and for man, and therefore has a responsibility not to shame him. Johnson expresses his own reserve when it comes to offering a definitive reading of this passage, but in the end, he prefers a hairstyle/hierarchical reading, acknowledging that if this is the voice of Paul, we cannot evade the tinge of patriarchy. Thus, he cannot in the end actually hold the two readings together. In Gundry-Volf's reading she draws out the many threads in the passage, both hierarchical and nonhierarchical, while at the same time arguing that, as they are *both* representative of Paul's thought, we should hold them together. As I noted previously, however, any reading of Paul that brings out even a soft patriarchy is in essence hierarchical and so should acknowledge the implications of the text for the position of women vis-à-vis men, Christ, and God, and how that is seen to be lived out.

One of the questions that we are faced with in this passage emerges clearly in this discussion. When confronted with the two strands of thought regarding men and women in 11:3–16, we have a number of exegetical options. We could choose to explain this as a dialectic in Paul's thought that he presents in order to give a full picture of the place of men and women in relation to God and to one another. We could choose to explain it on the basis of Paul's conflicting worlds, with the Corinthian shame/honor paradigm in tension with his "in the Lord" vision for humanity. On the other hand, we might perceive more of an uneasy tension between the two strands of thought if we are of the opinion that the two views of the relation of man to woman are somewhat incompatible, or we could regard these two views as mutually exclusive and, therefore, contradictory. In addition to this, we must make a decision regarding the theology of gender expressed in 11:3–10, and explain what Paul means by these verses. As we continue to explore different interpretations of the key words and verses, we will return to the question of which options provide a satisfactory explanation of the passage. The idea of a dialectic in Paul's thought (or views held in tension) is an admirable attempt to iron out what others see as the "illogicality" of Paul's argument, but does it resolve our problems? We are left in

32. Ibid., 194.
33. Ibid.

the end with what these commentators like to portray as a soft patriarchy or some "patriarchal connotations," rooted in creation, alongside a mutuality possibly rooted in creation as well or possibly in Paul's Christology and pneumatology, but is this a correct reading of this passage, and of Paul's theology in general? In later sections we will examine other arguments that critique this reading. Ultimately, the traditional approach to the text, so I shall argue, leaves the reader with very few options for rescuing Paul from misogyny, or inconsistency, or bad theology, or all three.

iv. Shame/honor and hairstyles: Payne

As I mentioned above, there are those who do not read Paul as referring to actual head coverings, but to hairstyles for both men and women. Blomberg claims that the literal translation of verse 4 is "having down from the head" rather than "with his head covered." Thus, it could be that Paul is not speaking of a head covering at all, but of hair length. Blomberg opts for the literal translation and argues that Paul is ruling that men should not have long hair on the grounds that long hair would be associated with homosexuality. Thus, appearances of homosexuality dishonor God.[34] Blomberg believes that Paul is warning the Corinthians about how they should wear their hair, whether long or short, and/or whether tied up or not. These are social signifiers that could potentially communicate all manner of sexual impropriety.

Phillip B. Payne is in general agreement with this argument. He believes that the key to 1 Corinthians 11:2–16 lies in understanding that there are two "crucial conventions regarding head coverings" and that most interpretations miss these—first, that "it was generally regarded as a disgrace for men to wear long, effeminate hair, because of its associations with homosexuality," and second, that in "Hellenistic, Roman, and Jewish cultures, for centuries preceding and following the time of Paul, virtually all of the portraiture, sculpture, and other graphic evidence depicts respectable women's hair done up, not let loose down."[35] Payne, then, identifies one of the most problematic issues with the head coverings argument. There was no *one* convention regarding head coverings in Corinth among the Romans, Greeks, and Jews that we can identify as the norm both for men and women with respect to signifiers for shame and honor.

34. Blomberg, *NIV Application Commentary,* 211.
35. Payne, "Wild Hair," 9.

In the course of arguing that 1 Corinthians 11:2–16 is referring to hair length and bound-up hair, Payne's argument undermines those who would argue for head coverings for women and no head coverings for men as a necessity for regarding propriety either in worship or more generally between the sexes. This rests on a number of observations, some with respect to head coverings in general, and some with respect to head coverings in a liturgical setting. With regard to the latter, it was not a disgrace at all for a man to have his head covered in worship in Graeco-Roman culture. Liturgical head coverings for men were common practice in Roman, Greek, and Jewish culture. Greek women, including women in prayer, were usually depicted without a garment covering the head; Jewish women would have covered their heads at all times in public, while both Roman men and women are depicted with head coverings when making a sacrifice.[36] Roman worship customs regarding a garment over the head made no distinction between the sexes.[37] Payne also points out that just as it was not a Greek custom for women to cover their heads when praying, neither was it disgraceful for a man to cover his head to pray, as that was the custom in Roman and Jewish piety. On the difference between Greek and Jewish liturgical practices, John Temple Bristow writes, "Greek men would have found the Jewish insistence upon wearing head coverings during worship strange if not distasteful."[38] It should also be noted that as well as Greek, Roman, and Jewish men and women having different practices, liturgical practices were not synonymous with general practices in society. In public, for example, a Roman man would uncover his head in front of a superior as a sign of respect. If we try to bring some unity to what was expected and why in a multicultural congregation in first-century Corinth, we will find ourselves in very muddy waters. In other words, if we wish to attribute that which is shameful solely to a cultural practice, we will find we have even more problems in providing a rationale for Paul's argument.[39]

36. Payne, *Man and Woman*, 152.

37. Ibid., 155.

38. Bristow, *What Paul Really Said about Women*, 81.

39. Edsall claims that there is now good evidence that head coverings for women were a widespread practice. He writes, "Importantly, recent scholarship on both Greek and Roman costume has concluded that women *did* wear veils, even if it was not a custom without exception," citing Olson, *Dress and the Roman Woman*, and Llewellyn-Jones, *Aphrodite's Tortoise*, in support of his thesis. He discusses this more in relation to women covering their heads in public as a general practice rather than a liturgical practice, but nevertheless, it may be that the practice of head coverings in Corinth was

Payne's final and interesting point against reading this as referring to head coverings is that "[t]he descriptions of hair in verses 14–15, 1 Tim 2:9, and 1 Peter 3:3 imply that there was no general church custom that women wear head-covering shawls."[40] In addition to this, if this is an apostolic ruling, it is unusual that it is not included in any other epistle. Finally, it is claimed that Paul's explicit reference to hair in verses 14–15 supports the hair length reading, and thus Payne concludes that a head covering reading is too problematic.

For these reasons, he opts for the hairstyle reading, and provides fourteen reasons to identify men's head covering with effeminate hair (and therefore homosexual behavior).[41] In his view, therefore, "effeminate hair symbolizes rejection of God's standards."[42] He then gives fourteen reasons to interpret women's "uncovered head" as referring to hair let down.[43] Payne, with Blomberg, believes that the disgrace was in the man having long hair, and that this was shameful because of the association with invitations to homosexual liaisons.[44] Similarly it was shameful for a woman to wear her hair down as that was only a practice among immoral or loose women, those eschewing marriage and embracing sexual promiscuity, or adultery.[45] Payne believes that the entire passage reflects Paul's view, but argues that what Paul is really saying is that women should wear their hair bound up and that men should keep their hair short, because that is the "nature of things." His conclusion is that a man looking like a woman will be inviting homosexual liaisons, and a woman defying her marriage vows is equally offensive. Claiming that Paul draws those arguments from creation ordinances, Payne argues that man and woman are created (equally) to procreate and thus any behavior that undermines the creation order is anathema to Paul. Payne claims that Paul has an egalitarian approach to men and women, and that his primary concern is that they should both avoid being associated with shameful behavior. His solution to the problem of what Paul means by the angels, Payne believes to be self-evident. "The obvious

---

more widespread than the hairstyles advocates have yet acknowledged. Edsall, "Greco-Roman Costume," 137.

40. Payne, "Wild Hair," 12.

41. Payne, *Man and Woman*, 144–45.

42. Ibid., 177.

43. Ibid., 166–67.

44. Payne, "Wild Hair," 11.

45. Ibid., 12.

reason for this appeal is that angels are present, observing the church (1 Tim. 5:21; Eph. 3:10; Rev. 1:20; 2:1, 8, 12, 18; 3:1, 7, 14) and should not be offended. Angels report to God what they see."[46] As we will note below, the question of who the angels are and why they might be offended, according to other scholars, is far from clear. Payne's reading is ostensibly a hairstyle/nonhierarchical reading, although as will become evident, he also draws out the patriarchal connotations, which must then undermine his insistence on an egalitarian reading.

v. Shame/honor and hairstyles: Murphy-O'Connor

Jerome Murphy-O'Connor is another advocate of a hairstyle/nonhierarchical reading, or "hairdos," as he calls them, in relation to shame and honor. Murphy-O'Connor's predominant theme is the need for differentiation between men and women. According to Murphy-O'Connor, Paul's main concern is that men and women should be seen to be different and that, on a practical level, modes of dress "should manifest, not obscure, this difference."[47] Like Payne, however, he believes that Paul is addressing issues of deviant sexuality, especially homosexual practice among men. He is convinced that long hair is the "self-advertising of the active homosexual, which Paul condemned in 1 Cor 6:9."[48] Similarly, if the women had untended hair, they may as well have look liked a man or a lesbian.[49] This, then, is a case of serious and offensive gender bending.

As with many a commentator, Murphy-O'Connor attempts to reconstruct a possible scenario that will make sense of Paul's comments, as he believes that if we can reconstruct the situation in Corinth, then we will understand the internal logic of the passage. One of the key suppositions for Murphy-O'Connor's argument is that Paul was deeply offended by long hair on a man. On the basis of verse 14, we can surmise that "[l]ong hair on a man did upset him badly."[50] Despite Murphy-O'Connor's assurance that this is a passage about hair length, his explanation does not paint Paul in a particularly good light, either as a theologian or a writer. Murphy-O'Connor is confident that his account of Paul's "logic" is correct,

46. Ibid., 13.
47. Murphy-O'Connor, *Keys*, 132.
48. Ibid., 139.
49. Ibid., 147–48.
50. Ibid., 144.

while at the same time admitting that the logic itself is not very convincing! This passage, he claims, is concerned with the difference between men and women and is limited exclusively to matters of dress. "Paul uses the Genesis narrative to serve his purpose. It appears to do so, but the logic is questionable."[51]

It is difficult to fathom whether we should view Paul as presenting a coherent or an incoherent argument, as opinions are so divided. Many commentators wish to give him the benefit of the doubt. So Murphy-O'Connor writes: "In writing 1 Cor 11:2–16, Paul was under a strain which naturally influenced his style. He did not have as much information as he would have wished, and he was uneasy at being obliged to deal with the surface of what could be a serious problem. Nonetheless, his control was such that he presents a perfectly coherent multi-pronged argument against hair arrangements which tended to blur the difference between the sexes."[52] Murphy-O'Connor proceeds to identify several features of Paul's argument and attempts to show how they constitute a coherent whole. These features are theological reasoning (vv. 7–9), the equality of women (vv. 10–12), an appeal to popular Stoic philosophy, which saw hair arrangements as something more than mere conventions (vv. 13–15), and finally that "men should look like men and women like women."[53] He concedes that Paul "may have reacted emotionally to the disregard of a convention that had changed and would change again, as did many at least twice in this century, when women started to bob their hair and men to let theirs grow long," but in his view, despite the many pressures and strains on Paul from the flagrant abuse of his authority and these deviant sexual practices, "he did not crumple into incoherence or lose his penetrating persuasiveness."[54] In an anodyne reading of Paul, the argument goes that he is simply exhorting men and women to behave with due respect and honor to one another as "different" before God, either through hairstyle or head coverings.

The argument between head coverings and hair length centers on the Greek term κατὰ κεφαλῆς in verse 4. Blomberg asserts that the literal translation is "having down *from* the head." Ben Witherington dismisses this reading and claims that verse 4 should be read as "having down *on* the head." Against Blomberg, Payne, and others, Witherington uncompromisingly

51. Ibid., 133.
52. Ibid., 156.
53. Ibid.
54. Ibid., 156–57.

asserts, "[t]he issue is headcoverings."[55] It is clear that scholarly opinion is divided on the matter. There is no clear consensus. We are driven then to examine the context in order to try to make sense of the meaning. If we are to take this text as representing Paul's own opinion, then, to some extent, both parties offer some convincing arguments. In my opinion, the head coverings explanation offered by Witherington, Fee, and Thiselton, among others is more convincing, for reasons which I will go on to explain. What we will go on to see, however, is that it may be possible to accommodate both views in some form. For now, we note that it is not possible to resolve the issue of the meaning of verse 4 once and for all, and so I propose that we bracket the debate and continue with the argument to see if we can follow the logic of Paul's thought through the passage. It will become clear that it is not necessary to identify the exact nature of the infringement to critique the logic of the passage, and the flow of the argument.

The Difficult Women

4 πᾶς ἀνὴρ προσευχόμενος ἢ προφητεύων κατὰ κεφαλῆς ἔχων καταισχύνει τὴν κεφαλὴν αὐτοῦ·

One of the unifying themes in most of the traditional arguments is that it is clearly the women who are causing the problems and, as such, are the target of Paul's rebuke. Payne, Murphy-O'Connor, and Thiselton protest against such readings, appealing, as they do, to an analogous rebuke for the men in verse 4. It is very difficult, however, perhaps even impossible, to argue for parity in Paul's treatment of men and women. There is a general consensus that although Paul is clearly addressing both men and women, the stronger rebuke is unequivocally reserved for the women. This is apparent in the fact that there is no penalty for the men if they defy Paul, whereas there is a harsh penalty/threat suggested for any obstinate women. As we have noted, all interpreters of this passage will have an imagined scenario in Corinth in view. One factor to note when assessing a possible reading is what has already been decided on in respect of the behavior of the men and the behavior of the women, and how it is assumed that Paul would be reacting to this behavior.

As we have noted, Fee and Thiselton believe that the Corinthian women were taking as a "right" what was given to them by Paul as a freedom (to pray and prophesy). Their freedom became a license for their bad behavior,

55. Witherington, *Conflict and Community in Corinth*, 232.

and the catalyst to their serious overstepping of the mark. In other words, they were behaving badly in response to Paul's own teaching in the first place. Payne suggests further that the women would have been letting their hair down "for the same reason it was popular in the Dionysiac cult," and so explains their behavior as a blend of cultural and theological influences. On the one hand, he writes, "[g]iven the extent of the Dionysiac influence in Corinth, it is easy to imagine some women thinking, 'Hey, let's have some fun and let our hair down in church!'" On the other, "It is not surprising that some women *who exulted in their freedom in Christ* would express that freedom by letting their hair down just as the Dionysiacs did." According to Payne, the blend of freedom in Christ (essentially a good thing) and pagan influence (essentially a bad thing) is the cause of their bad behavior. He adds, however, that even if they were being influenced by the Dionysiac cult that this "would not necessarily entail accepting the bad things associated with [it]."[56] Just to add to the blend of ideas that Payne is offering as to precisely *why* these women were doing what they were doing, he concludes that due to the Corinthians' spiritualized and overly realized eschatology, "it is easy to imagine women in Corinth thinking they were in the new age like the angels and could express their freedom in Christ by letting their hair down."[57] The level of speculation here is extremely high, and as I will note below, this view of the women rests on the assumption that despite the fact that their freedom led them to behave in ways that gave the appearance of immorality (in the eyes of the church and of society at large), they continued to behave in such ways, not seeming to care what it looked like.

Imagine That!

All interpreters are forced to speculate to some extent. As we have noted, there are some who attempt to argue that the bad behavior (in Paul's eyes) is shared equally between the men and the women. We have already considered Murphy-O'Connor's attempts to lay blame equally at the feet of men and women. Richard Hays is another who finds fault with both sexes. Hays speculates that Paul's own teaching or catechesis "may have led them to express unity in Christ in terms of the erasure of traditional signs of gender" so both men and women are guilty of rejecting signs of differentiation.[58]

---

56. Payne, *Man and Woman*, 169.

57. Ibid., 170–71.

58. Hays, *First Corinthians*, 182–83, cited in Thiselton, *Corinthians*, 106–7.

Is Paul just referring to men and women rejecting signs of differentiation? Are the women wild because of Paul's teaching, because of pagan influence, or because of bad Corinthian theology? And what about the men? What are the reasons for *their* bad behavior? Why are they putting head coverings on when they should be leaving them off, or growing their hair long (in hope of a gay liaison?) when they should be keeping it short? When reading accounts of historical reconstructions, we are often told that "it is easy to imagine" this or that. It is not always clear, however, what we are being asked to imagine. If we think, for example, that Paul is referring to a real and not a hypothetical situation with the men,[59] it is not clear whether we are to imagine that the leaders were forcing men to wear head coverings, or that the men in the *ekklesia* were wearing head coverings in opposition to the leaders. Or, might they have been growing their hair, either wanting to appear gay, or not caring whether they did? Each reading yields a particular picture of the church in Corinth. Despite attempts to paint a picture of equal blame, most scholars in the end agree that it is *primarily* the women who are behaving badly, and that Paul is targeting them in this passage.

The dominant picture among scholars is a version of the following: Christian women converts who have been brought up in a blatantly misogynist society, freed by their newfound relationship with Jesus Christ into a reconstituted way of relating to the world, to men, and to one another, taught by Paul that in Christ there is no longer a superior/inferior relationship between male and female, licensed by Paul to pray and prophesy, and invited even to lead, have been corrupted, and are beginning to behave in disgraceful ways. In this newfound existence, initially encouraged by Paul, they have veered into shameful (even disgusting) practices. This may be understandable as there were cults around at the time in which women did indeed behave in this way (e.g., the Dionysiacs). It may be that they were even whipping themselves into a wild charismatic frenzy. Whatever the reason, they had thrown all caution to the wind, not caring who they shamed—themselves, their fathers, husbands, sons, uncles, God, Christ, and the angels. They ceased to care what they looked like and what their appearance conveyed to the outside world. They ceased to care whether they were being seen to be behaving like prostitutes and adulterers in a worship service. If such an account of the situation is reasonably accurate, we have to then consider how the men were responding. There are three possible

---

59. See Fee, *First Epistle*, 505. Fee posits that Paul is referring to a hypothetical situation among the men in order to make his point.

options. The first is that the men were colluding and joining in with their own version of bad behavior (i.e., covering their heads or growing their hair long). Thus, it had become a problem that had "infected" the entire church. The second is that they were overlooking the offense, not realizing the seriousness of what was happening, hence Paul's intervention. The third is that the men had tried to correct their womenfolk but they would not listen to their fathers, their husbands, their church leaders, and possibly even some fellow women, who had presumably pleaded with them not to behave so badly in public. They were in need of discipline from the apostle himself. We are required to imagine here that what they were doing was so bad that Paul insisted on intervening. The seriousness of the situation, on Payne's account, may be attributed to the moral link between hair let down and adultery or prostitution. Others make the link between throwing off head coverings and this offensive, shameful behavior. The issue is not yet resolved among commentators. The seriousness of the behavior is spelled out, however, in verse 6.

The Whores of Corinth?

6 εἰ γὰρ οὐ κατακαλύπτεται γυνή, καὶ κειράσθω· εἰ δὲ αἰσχρὸν γυναικὶ τὸ κείρασθαι ἢ ξυρᾶσθαι, κατακαλυπτέσθω.

Supposedly, Paul goes on to say either,

> For if a woman will not veil herself, then she should cut off her hair; but if it is disgraceful for a woman to have her hair cut off or to be shaved, she should wear a veil. (NRSV)

or,

> For if a woman does not cover her head, she might as well have her hair cut off; but if it is a disgrace for a woman to have her hair cut off or her head shaved, then she should cover her head. (NIV)

or,

> For if a woman does not cover her head, let her also have her hair cut off; but if it is disgraceful for a woman to have her hair cut off or her head shaved, let her cover her head. (NAS)

or,

> For if the woman be not covered, let her also be shorn: but if it be a
> shame for a woman to be shorn or shaven, let her be covered. (KJV)

There are various ways of reading this verse, as can be seen above. Thiselton attempts to soften the reading by pointing out that the verbs are in the middle voice, indicating a reflexive action. She should cut her (own) hair. This clearly takes the edge off any implication that "she should be shorn"! Others point out that Paul is sometimes prone to strong language to make a point (as in Gal 5:12) and that this is an example of Pauline hyperbole simply serving to reinforce the idea that being uncovered is shameful. We could paraphrase an anodyne reading in the following way:

If a woman is intent on shaming her "head" (her own head and man/her husband) by throwing off her head covering or letting down her hair, she may as well go the whole way and just cut off her hair, but if/as that is equally shameful, she should remain covered.

Other interpretations, however, might bring out the possibility of a threat or even a punishment.

If a woman does not cover her head, she should have her head shaved. She is flagrantly disgracing herself and man/her husband, and so should be made an example of with a sign of public disgrace. But as this is equally shameful, she should be covered.

There are those who attempt to take the underlying force out of this statement by arguing for a gentler reading, or arguing that Paul is simply using hyperbole to make a point. Bruce Winter, however, in his sociological study of the Corinthian world, brings out the impact of these verses, highlighting the sign of the shorn or shaved woman as one who has been punished by being publicly shamed. He writes:

> Paul made a startling statement about the unveiled wife. He said that her behaviour was "one and the same thing as a woman who has been shorn" (11.5). It is known, e.g., that in Cyprus the law prescribed that "a woman guilty of adultery shall have her hair cut off and be a prostitute," i.e., like a foreigner or freedwoman who provided sexual favours at a dinner. Therefore Paul equated not wearing a veil with the social stigma of a publicly exposed and punished adulteress reduced to the status of a prostitute.[60]

60. Winter, *After Paul*, 128.

He carries on, expressing surprise at Paul's imperative in 11:6a that if a woman publicly dishonors her husband then she ought to bear the public stigma. He goes on to note, correctly, "Paul then argued the converse, that if it was shameful for a wife to be shorn or shaven, then the only alternative was to wear the marriage veil" (11:6c).[61] Winter also notes that the use of ὀφείλει (ought) in 11:2-16 invokes "the most powerful argument that could be used in correcting conduct in the first century."[62]

Payne's work on Paul attempts to interpret Paul as one who is extremely favorable towards women, emphasizing again and again the evidence in Paul's writings for Paul's own inclusion of women in ministry, friendship, leadership, etc. He too however, does not avoid the punitive overtones of this verse, and searching for a universal motif for shame and honor, makes the following point in relation to the shorn head. The shorn adulteress is paralleled in non-Jewish customs. Payne cites Tacitus (AD 98) on a German custom regarding adultery: "Punishment is prompt and is the husband's prerogative: her hair close-cropped, stripped of her clothes, her husband drives her from his house in presence of his relatives and pursues her with blows through the length of the village."[63]

Winter himself finds references to these practices to be "startling" and "surprising," but the impact of Paul alluding to them is surely more serious. If we take this to be the voice of Paul then we must face up to the coercive nature of his statement. Regardless of the infraction (bareheadedness or wild hair), Paul is recommending here that women who pray and prophesy unveiled/loose-haired should be treated by the community in the same way that they used to treat whores and adulterers. One might argue that he was using forceful language simply to enforce his point, however, it remains shockingly forceful language. First, it emphasizes the extent of the shameful behavior, and second, we cannot escape the fact that women are under a threat while men are not. It is the women, not the men, who are behaving in this shocking way and who are deserving of being shamed by their own community. With this in mind, let us turn to the descriptions of the relationship of men to God and men to women in the next section of the text.

61. Ibid., 128-29.

62. Ibid., 130-31.

63. Tacitus, *Dialogus, Agricola, Germania*, 290-91 (Peterson, LCL), cited in Payne, *Man and Woman*, 172.

TWO

Men and Women before God

In this chapter, we will question the more moderate readings of Paul, drawing out the implications of his theology of gender expressed in 11:3–10. We will also begin to examine the implications of the various arguments for the church today, pressing them to their own logical conclusions should we see the need to apply these truths to current church practice.

The Glory of Man: Culture or Creation?

7 ἀνὴρ μὲν γὰρ οὐκ ὀφείλει κατακαλύπτεσθαι τὴν κεφαλήν, εἰκὼν καὶ δόξα θεοῦ ὑπάρχων· ἡ γυνὴ δὲ δόξα ἀνδρός ἐστιν. 8 οὐ γάρ ἐστιν ἀνὴρ ἐκ γυναικός, ἀλλὰ γυνὴ ἐξ ἀνδρός· 9 καὶ γὰρ οὐκ ἐκτίσθη ἀνὴρ διὰ τὴν γυναῖκα, ἀλλὰ γυνὴ διὰ τὸν ἄνδρα. 10 διὰ τοῦτο ὀφείλει ἡ γυνὴ ἐξουσίαν ἔχειν ἐπὶ τῆς κεφαλῆς διὰ τοὺς ἀγγέλους.

7 For a man ought not to have his head veiled, since he is the image and reflection of God; but woman is the reflection of man. 8 Indeed, man was not made from woman, but woman from man. 9 Neither was man created for the sake of woman, but woman for the sake of man. 10 For this reason a woman ought to have a symbol of authority on her head, because of the angels. (NRSV)

7 A man ought not to cover his head, since he is the image and glory of God; but woman is the glory of man. 8 For man did not come from woman, but woman from man; 9 neither was man created for woman,

but woman for man. **10** It is for this reason that a woman ought to have authority over her own head, because of the angels. (NIV)

Those who argue that the shame/honor paradigm alluded to in verse 4 is encoded in cultural signs have to acknowledge that Paul either shifts or blends his argument to argue that the shame/honor paradigm is (also?) encoded in the God-ordained difference between man and woman's relation to God and to one another. Many commentators note a shift or oscillation in Paul's argumentation. Michael Lakey writes, "Paul oscillates back and forth from theology (v. 3), to implicit paraenesis regarding honour and attire (vv. 4–6), to cosmogony and anthropology (vv. 7–9), to explicit paraenesis regarding attire (v. 10), to anthropology and generation (vv. 11–12), to attire (v. 13) and to nature and custom (vv. 14–16)."[1] So in verses 7–9 we are moving into what Lakey calls "cosmogony and anthropology." Thus, there are two difficulties with these verses. The first pertains to the apparent shift in thinking and the second to the claim that man alone or man first is the "image and glory" of God.

The "shift in thinking" only occurs if it is true that Paul is referring to culture in the first place. There are several reasons, however, why it is hard to sustain the argument that Paul is concerned principally with a cultural issue. First, we have noted the almost impossible task of identifying which cultural practices he is referring to that would be universally shaming for both men and women in relation to head coverings. Second, we have noted the seriousness of the practices and the harsh nature of his rebuke. Third, he begins the passage, in verse 3, with a reference to man's and woman's relation to one another, to Christ, and to God, a theme which he appears to pick up again in verse 7. I will return to verse 3 in due course. For now, it will suffice to note that the evidence for Paul's argument as rooted solely in a particular view of creation rather than culture is very strong.

There have been numerous studies on the meaning of "head" (κεφαλὴ) in verse 3, which I will come to in more detail in chapter 4. As I am attempting in this section to study Paul's method in order to show that Paul's argument is predicated on a theological and not a cultural premise, I simply wish to note for now how easily Paul elides the literal and metaphorical use of the term "head." If man behaves in a certain way in respect of his physical head, he will shame his metaphorical "head" (i.e., Christ). If woman behaves in a certain way in respect of her physical head, she will shame

1. Lakey, *Image and Glory of God,* 146.

45

her metaphorical "head" (i.e., man). Paul is claiming that clothing/attire, appearances, what we bear on our physical heads, has a profound spiritual and metaphysical significance in respect to gender relations to one another and to God. There is no escaping this principle. Paul's argument is not one that is rooted in cultural symbol, but a principle that is rooted in theological signification. He does not start in one place and move to another; he interweaves one with another. The question is, which came first? If we want to argue for a cultural/creational rationale, then we have to posit one of two logical sequences (a and b below) that rest on a particular premise—*viz.* that Paul views his own cultural norms (either hairstyles or head coverings) as having some sort of enduring theological significance, presumably because he understands them to be inextricably linked to the creation order. This is a possible reading and could be backed up by verse 14 regarding the very "nature of things." So, regardless of the fact that they are simply cultural mores, Paul has invested them with deep theological significance. The question thus arises: is this (a) because he believes those cultural signifiers have been ordained by God in the first place, or (b) because he believes they exist simply to reflect what has been ordained by God? If (a) then we should consider continuing to follow these rulings in the church (if we can establish what the rulings are in the first place). If (b) we should continue to seek culturally relevant signifiers to reflect the creation order and distinction in respect of male and female order and relations. I will explain below how (b) might work if we think that is the right response.

Attempts to unify the cultural/creational codes in Paul's thought without acknowledging these problems merely result in the claim that Paul undergoes various "shifts" in his thinking without really giving us a satisfactory answer as to why. In the end, it can only result in a claim that he has a patriarchal and hierarchical view of creation on the one hand, and a mutual view of men and women and their equality in Christ and in the Spirit or "in the Lord" on the other. One of the problems with this, however, is that in verses 11–12 Paul uses the phrase "in the Lord," which could be an appeal to a new order "in Christ," but then also goes on to paint a picture of man and woman as interdependent in terms of origin, thus creation. This is a very strong argument for the de facto interdependence of man and woman, thus strengthening the view that Paul is simply being contradictory. Moreover, these accounts have to explain how Paul understands the relationship of cultural practice to theological principle. Either Paul believes that cultural practices regarding gender distinction are rooted in creation, in which case we should continue with these practices today, or we have to find another solution. If the former is the case, regardless of whether we see this as head coverings or hairstyle then if we wish to transmute the sign into a contemporary equivalent, we must be sure of Paul's argument in the first place. As I will attempt to demonstrate below, this is much more problematic than many will acknowledge. The challenge is to find a sign that will express the theological significance of the idea that "man is the glory of God, and woman is the glory of man" with what C. S. Peirce calls an "iconic" signifier; one that has a direct relation to the thing signified.[2] The reason for this is what we see in the Corinthian letter is a spiritual truth either applied to or extrapolated out of a cultural practice that is directly linked to the part of the body to which the metaphor is applied.

Both Payne and Hays attempt to apply this passage to our own time by suggesting equivalent transcultural signs in contemporary culture, but first we have to be convinced of their interpretation of Paul's understanding of the signification of the head covering for women and the bare head for men, and then we have to be convinced of the modern equivalent of this sign. If their premise is faulty or if they cease to maintain the signification expressed in Paul's teaching adequately then these attempts will fail. Payne's interpretation of the transcultural message of his interpretation of Paul is: "Don't use your freedom in Christ as an excuse to dress in a way that is sexually suggestive or subversive. Keep it clean!" He then seeks to apply this principle to modern modes of dress, but adds the disclaimer: while we may implement these restrictions among church members, "[t]his is not applicable to sinners who walk through our doors." These restrictions should not be used to exclude sinners.[3] This sounds highly problematic. Payne's argument is dependent on a very particular interpretation of verses 3–16, and one which has not yet been adequately demonstrated. Similarly, Hays argues that we might understand this principle in Paul as equivalent to wearing a baseball cap to a formal dinner. It is perceived as "rude and irreverent," "a breach of etiquette," and "constitutes attention-seeking behavior which thereby dishonors God and shames the self."[4] The fact that Hays mentions a modern-day head covering (a baseball cap) is beguilingly misleading. Ostensibly it appears reasonable that he has found a modern-day head covering sign in a particular cultural setting that communicates

2. For Peircean semiotics see Peirce, *Selected Writings*.

3. Payne, *Man and Woman*, 214.

4. Hays, *First Corinthians*, 84, cited in Thiselton, *The First Epistle*, 828.

disrespect. This, however, is a category error and fails to take into account (a) the seriousness of the women's infringement (for a man to wear a baseball cap to a formal dinner would surely not result in a punishment as serious as Paul seems to be advocating), (b) the significance of the physical head in relation to the spiritual head, and (c) the assumption within Paul's writing that he is referring to universal signifiers. Most attempts to find contemporary equivalents fail to do justice either to the seriousness of the infringement, the cosmological implications of the infringement, and the theological grounding of Paul's alleged argument. To transmute both the meaning and the sign into another practice requires a complex series of steps which I will spell out in more detail in the section on κεφαλὴ below.

Many years ago, Chrysostom made all the obvious links that emerge from the passage, and he follows the logic perfectly. First he clarifies the meaning of the sign, and why precisely the error of wearing the wrong sign was so egregious.

> Symbols many and diverse have been given both to man and woman; to him of rule, to her of subjection: and among them this also, that she should be covered, while he hath his head bare. If now these be symbols you see that both err when they disturb the proper order, and transgress the disposition of God, and their own proper limits, both the man falling into the woman's inferiority, and the woman rising up against the man by her outward habiliments. For if exchange of garments be not lawful, so that neither she should be clad with a cloak, nor he with a mantle or a veil: ("for the woman," saith He, "shall not wear that which pertaineth to a man, neither shall a man put on a woman's garments:") much more is it unseemly for these (Deut. xxii. 5.) things to be interchanged. [5]

He then correctly observes the inextricable link between the cultural codes and the God-ordained codes from which Paul is constructing his argument, and having made the link, shows why it is precisely this that determines the nature of the sin.

> For the former indeed were ordained by men, even although God afterwards ratified them: but this by nature, I mean the being covered or uncovered. But when I say Nature, I mean God. For He it is Who created Nature. When therefore thou overturnest these boundaries, see how great injuries ensue. And tell me not this, that the error is but small. For first, it is great even of itself: being as it is disobedience. Next, though it were small, it became great because

5. Chrysostom, *Homilies on the Epistles of Paul to the Corinthians*, 26.4.

of the greatness of the things whereof it is a sign. However, that it is a great matter, is evident from its ministering so effectually to good order among mankind, the governor and the governed being regularly kept in their several places by it. So that he who transgresseth disturbs all things, and betrays the gifts of God, and casts to the ground the honor bestowed on him from above; not however the man only, but also the woman. For to her also it is the greatest of honors to preserve her own rank; as indeed of disgraces, the behavior of a rebel. Wherefore he laid it down concerning both, thus saying, Ver. 4. "Every man praying or prophesying having his head covered, dishonoreth his head. But every woman praying or prophesying with her head unveiled dishonoreth her head."[6]

Chrysostom is clear that the codes of dress advocated by Paul are God-given signs of the place of both men and women in creation, and that to throw them off is a serious transgression. Man holds the superior position and woman the subordinate one. Man the governor, woman the governed. Both are honored in maintaining those boundaries. Both reflect those positions in their attire. (In a later citation from Chrysostom we will note that he perceives this order of super- and sub-ordination to be a result of the Fall, not to have been established at creation.) Modern commentators often shy away from such an interpretation, claiming, as we have seen, that Paul's theology of gender is one of mutuality and respect within difference. This is because they see evidence for this latter view in verses 11–16, and so attempt to make sense of Paul's theology of gender in verses 3–10 in the light of what follows. Does Paul have a gendered theology that is based on difference, mutuality, and respect, or a gendered theology of hierarchy—superiority and inferiority and/or preeminence and derivation? Chrysostom assumes the latter, giving a justifiable exegesis. If we agree with Chrysostom's perspicacious comments, then we might possibly want to follow Lakey in his response when he notes that "the generative codes of this passage are, from the perspective of current readers, aberrant and implausible." Lakey's conclusion in the light of this is that we cannot be constrained by them in an identical fashion.[7] In other words, he would give up on trying to find a modern equivalent sign, as this is just not the way we view men and women anymore. It seems clear that if we take the whole of the passage to represent Paul's own thought then we have to accept that,

6. Ibid.

7. Lakey, *Image and Glory*, 181.

quite strangely, he invested a cultural sign with a theological significance, presumably because he believed that sign to have been ordained by God in the first place, as Chrysostom notes. Not only this, but that these signs have been introduced as signs of man as the one who governs and woman as the one who is governed. This then raises some serious questions for the church in relation to the teachings of Paul. Are we going to ignore this passage altogether? Are we not actually doing that anyway? If we are not making sure that women are wearing head coverings, or keeping their hair long and tied up, and that men are keeping their hair short, are we just tacitly sidelining Paul and his teaching? What other verses do we treat in this way and why? How do we differentiate between what we should be adhering to and what we can quietly ignore? The questions that this passage raises in relation to practices in the church have not been adequately answered yet.

Man as God's Glory

Let us turn to some other knotty problems in relation to the phrase that man is the "image and glory" of God. What is not yet clear is quite what Paul means by stating that man ought not to cover his head since he is the "image" and "glory" of God, and that woman is man's glory. I will give examples of three readings here to demonstrate the diversity of opinion about how this statement should be read. The first is from Gundry-Volf, who finds in Paul the strongest possible reciprocal emphasis as we have already noted, focusing on the gender distinction, but not hierarchy.

> Paul's main point is that man and woman are both the *glory of another* and therefore have an obligation not to cause shame to their "heads" . . . since they are the glory of *different* persons—man is the glory of God, and woman is the glory of man—they must use different means to avoid shaming their "heads." But Paul appeals to creation to show their obligation to bring glory—each to the particular one whose glory they are by creation—which they do through distinctive masculine and feminine hairstyles [or head coverings].[8]

The second is from Payne and is an illustration of the "soft" patriarchy that I have alluded to above.

8. Gundry-Volf, "Gender and Creation," 157.

> First Corinthians 11:7c affirms that woman, not another man, is the glory of man. The glory of someone is the person in whom he glories, as the man glories over the woman in Gen 2:23. Woman is depicted as the crowning glory of creation made specifically to be man's partner. Most men would agree that of all creation, woman is the most beautiful. The history of art typically exalts woman as the fairest of God's creation. Adam's "glorifying" in the first woman is immediately followed by 2:24, "For this reason a man will leave his father and mother and be united to his wife." . . . When husbands treat their wives as their glory, marriage is beautiful.[9]

It may be that some women would appreciate being named as the "crowning glory" of creation. (I am not at all sure what to make of the appeal to "all men" to agree that of all creation, woman is the most beautiful.) However, reciprocity fades from view. "Each of these specific affirmations is a good reason for a wife to show respect to her husband: man is the image and glory of God (v. 7b), woman is the glory of man (v. 7c), woman's source was from man (v. 8), and woman was created to fulfill man (v. 9)."[10] Man fulfills a particular role in relation to God, woman in relation to man. In my opinion, this is truer to the text. One of the questions we must ask of this view, however, is whether this is the correct view of creation.

In order to answer this question, we need to define how we understand what Paul means by his use of "man." This, however, is not uncomplicated. Is he referring to prelapsarian man, fallen man, man "in Christ," or eschatological man? Fallen man is generally ruled out on the grounds of Romans 3:23 that all have sinned and fall short of the "glory" of God, which leaves us with the other exegetical options. Murphy-O'Connor believes that glory here is referring to the glory of both prelapsarian man and the glory that believers have in Christ, an eschatological glory that is already ours.[11] He holds that Paul does not believe in the inferiority of women because of what he later writes in verse 12 and that Paul "uses the variation in the mode of creation to prove simply that God intended men and women to be different." The meaning of δόξα (glory) therefore, in Murphy-O'Connor's view, is not relevant to Paul's argument.[12]

Attempts to read this verse as a benign message that men and women are simply different, or that women are creation's crowning glory, or that

9. Payne, *Man and Woman*, 179.

10. Ibid., 181.

11. Murphy-O'Connor, *Keys*, 134.

12. Ibid., 154.

both women and men are glorious, just in different ways, are not satisfacto-ry. Nor can we simply regard the verse as irrelevant, as Murphy-O'Connor suggests. It is not satisfactory either to attempt to "balance" this text by holding the creation account together with the "in the Lord" account, nor to override it with what succeeds this passage in verse 11–16. These read-ings overlook the fact that Paul is, in fact, reinterpreting Genesis 1:26–27 (presumably in the light of Genesis 2:22–23) because he believes that the male has a preeminent role in creation through which the female's relation-ship to God is either mediated or reflected. We cannot avoid the fact that Paul changes the wording of Genesis 1:26–27 from "image and likeness" to "image and glory" and then, against the Genesis 1 account that God's image and likeness is embodied in humanity (male *and female*), ascribes these new attributes solely to the male. It is not only the Genesis 1 account of creation that undermines a theology of the preeminence of the male, but also Genesis 4:1, where Eve declares, "With the help of the Lord, I have created a man."

It is not at all unusual to find commentaries in which the inferiority of women is deduced from this passage. Charles Hodge, after stating that he believes the author's thought remains somewhat obscure, continues,

> [t]he central idea must be that the woman, being taken from man, is inferior to him. It is even truer that she was created because of man, which means that the purpose of her existence is not in herself. Further according to the Genesis narrative, to which the Apostle alludes, the woman is expressly the man's helper . . . which underlines her inferior position. All of this reasoning must have deeply displeased the Corinthian feminists.[13]

It is common to find older commentaries echoing Hodge's reading. However, it is also common to find contemporary commentators (against Gundry-Volf et al.) perceiving the same thought expressed here in 1 Cor-inthians, although on the whole they tend now to be more critical of Paul. In other words, they see the same message of the inferiority of women to men that older readers saw, but they now find it unacceptable. My point is that Paul has left himself wide open to a reading of 1 Corinthians that is in direct contrast to Genesis 1 and Genesis 4, and utterly dismissive of woman's place in creation. Lakey brings out the implications of Paul's read-ing of Genesis in a particular way, which I have quoted at length because it

---

13. Hodge, *An Exposition to the First Epistle,* 106.

is important that it is expressed in his own words, including his critique of Paul at the end of this passage:

> The term εἰκών alludes to the first creation account and constitutes a biblical warrant for Paul's claim that man is δόξα θεοῦ. That Paul identifies man as δόξα θεοῦ in contradistinction to woman as δόξα ἀνδρός (v. 7b) is a clear indication that he regards the former epithet as a uniquely male trait. This indicates that he understands Genesis 1:26–27 to designate man but not woman, despite the story mentioning the creation of "male and female" (ἄρσεν καὶ θῆλυ LXX). Consequently, even if, as some commentators have suggested, Paul understands the primal human of Genesis 1 to have been androgynous, this reading suggests a peculiarly *male* form of androgyny. It remains unclear how Paul derives the expression εἰκὼν καὶ δόξα θεοῦ (1 Cor. 11:7) from Genesis 1:26–27, when the epithets used in the LXX version are εἰκὼν and ὁμοίωσις? That there is a relationship is clear from the twofold nature of the designations—"image and glory" mirroring "image and likeness." It may be that δόξα is an interpretative gloss on one or other of the terms used in the biblical story. However, since it is a poor rendering of both εἰκὼν and ὁμοίωσις, this is hardly satisfactory.[14]

Lakey's critique is apposite. So what do we make of Paul's claim that man is the image and glory of God? Is it possible to read this in any way that does not radically change the Genesis account? Lakey believes that Paul believes that "the male is the bearer of the divine likeness and a (now-lost) visible glory. . . . If Paul has Adam's luminescence in mind, then his argument here would be that male heads ought to be uncovered because the primal male as glory bearer was physically constituted for *revelation*, hence *visibility*. As such, male uncovering would be a creational norm."[15] As he also points out, and as he puts very succinctly, the woman is not the εἰκὼν of anyone. And so he concludes:

> Put bluntly: that the woman is δόξα ἀνδρός means she is not δόξα θεοῦ. This itself is sufficient to warrant the covering directive (v. 10); if man as δόξα θεοῦ is created to manifest the glory of God by uncovering, then, for Paul, woman as δόξα ἀνδρός is not. Perhaps he regards that which is not δόξα θεοῦ as deficient, with female covering as a remedy effected in the interests of her participation. Alternatively, it may be that what is not δόξα θεοῦ is out

14. Lakey, *Image and Glory*, 111.
15. Ibid.

of place and must be concealed in the interests of congregational purity. If so, then the irony of defining the ἐκκλεσία as male space, while simultaneously veiling man's glory is lost on Paul. Finally, it may be that "in God's presence [the glory of man] must inevitably turn to shame," and that in order thereby to authorize her ministry the prophesying woman must cover herself.[16]

Lakey is correct in his assessment of the rationale for head coverings/ hairstyles: "that the woman is δόξα ἀνδρός means she is not δόξα θεοῦ. This itself is sufficient to warrant the covering directive (v. 10)" This reading of Paul's distortion of Genesis 1:26–27 is markedly different from Stephen Dempster's reading of the same passage in which he gives his own interpretation of Genesis 1 in relation to the role of humanity in creation applied equally to man and woman and thus, all men and all women.

> Finally, the terminology used to describe the human beings shows this anthropological focus. The use of the terms "image" (*tselem*) and "likeness" (*demuth*) to describe humanity constitutes it as unique among the creatures. Much has been written about these words in the history of exegesis, but in their immediate context it is clear that they indicate that humanity is uniquely related to both God and the created order. Furthermore, these terms are relational and referential: humans are referential creatures; their being automatically signifies God. Since they are like God, they are best suited for a unique relationship to God, and this means that they also have a unique relation to their natural environment.[17]

Lakey's reading of Paul is entirely justifiable based on the text. One of the difficulties of this is that it makes for an extremely uncomfortable reading of Paul. Not only this, but it raises further problems regarding what Paul then goes on to claim in 1 Corinthians 11:12, which is an entirely different picture of man and woman in relation to one another and to God than that presented in 11:2–10. "For just as the woman came from the man [see Gen 2:23], so also the man through the woman [see Gen 4:1] and both from God." The idea that woman is taken "out of" man from Genesis 2:23 is given as the foundation for the unitive and indissoluble nature of marriage, with no hint of subordination. The fact that man is inevitably born of woman is the basis for mutual interdependence, and is not only a new "Christian" perspective but can be found in Genesis 4:1. Verses 11–16 then

16. Ibid., 112.

17. Dempster, *Dominion and Dynasty*, 57–58.

present not only a new Christian perspective, but a truer reading of Genesis than verses 2–10.[18]

A Sign of Authority

[10] διὰ τοῦτο ὀφείλει ἡ γυνὴ ἐξουσίαν ἔχειν ἐπὶ τῆς κεφαλῆς διὰ τοὺς ἀγγέλους.

[10] For this reason a woman ought to have a symbol of authority on her head, because of the angels.

The question of whose authority is in view and how it functions is yet another highly problematic matter. Is the head covering a sign of a woman's God-given authority, an authorization (by God? by men? by no one in particular?), a sign of subjection and subordination, a protection (against the angels?), or a prevention of some infringement? Many commentators take this verse to mean that a woman must have a sign of authority over her because she is inferior. Barclay makes the link between shame and subordination explicit. He writes, "the veil is *always a sign of subjection*, worn by an inferior in the presence of a superior; now woman is inferior to man, in the sense that man is head of the household; therefore it is wrong for a man to appear at public worship veiled and equally wrong for a woman to appear unveiled."[19] Barclay points out that it marks both a sign of inferiority *and* protection against shame.[20]

Lakey writes, "Notions of shame and honour implicit in this code situate females in a socially subordinate place to males" even if the veil signals authorization. "To illuminate the disparity, one needs only to observe that males require no equivalent marker of authorization (v. 7). Accordingly, I favour Martin's interpretation; covering authorizes female speech, but only insofar as it somehow corresponds to subordinate female nature."[21] He later adds that he follows Stuckenbruck "in regarding female covering as at least partially prophylactic; she covers because she has the potential to occasion

---

18. I owe this point to Matthew Lynch.

19. Barclay, *The Letter*, 114 (my italics).

20. Ibid., 115.

21. Lakey, *Image and Glory*, 110.

a cosmic boundary violation, to which both human males and angelic participants are liable."[22]

Others, however, are equally certain that this sign of authority is the woman's own authority to pray and prophesy, with no hint of subordination. Fitzmyer believes that Paul is referring to the fact that the woman exercises control over her own head. The head covering is a sign "of the power received from the Lord (v. 11) and of the dignity she has to worship and praise God in the presence of the angels, as the Greek prep. phrase that follows in this verse suggests."[23] Thiselton asserts that the veil constitutes a "badge of honour" signifying sexual reserve, "and hence of mastery of the self." He believes that this picks up Pauline themes from elsewhere in the letter. "Our point is that this theme of self-discipline which foregoes 'right' dominates 8:1—11:1, including especially 9:23–27, even with additional resonances in ch. 7."[24] In his view, Paul's injunction that women should be covered is entirely acceptable on the grounds that "public worship was neither the occasion for women to become 'objects' of attraction to be 'sized up' by men" nor "an occasion for women to offer cryptic 'suggestions' to men."[25] Note however that his argument transitions from one cause to another. He first argues that the covering is most certainly a sign of mastery of the self, implying that it has some kind of empowering signification, to then arguing that it is really a protection for both women and men from provocative symbols and lustful thoughts respectively, to concluding finally that as women's clothing honors their men, "women's clothing has an impact on the status of men."[26] We are back to the unavoidable conclusion that what women wear on their heads is significant because women must be respectful in order to protect the status of men. There is no reciprocity. Men for their part must be respectful in their attire in order to honor Christ primarily. It is only in honoring Christ that they honor women.[27] This is an important distinction.

22. Ibid., 113.

23. Fitzmyer, *First Corinthians*, 417.

24. Thiselton, *The First Epistle*, 802.

25. Ibid., 801–2.

26. Ibid., 802.

27. Lakey interprets this verse in the following way: "Female unveiling as boundary transgression is certainly intelligible in terms of Paul's biblical etiology of gender, since, although a created good (Gen. 2:18–25), the first woman remains associated with transgression in this etiological tradition by virtue of the fall story (Gen. 3:1–7). This association is clear in Tertullian: 'you are the devil's gateway: you are the unsealer of that

Some Stranger Readings

As an indication of how these verses lend themselves to speculation and how they have been the subject of some more unusual interpretations, I will give two examples of this in Pauline scholarship. The first is an earlier reading by Murphy-O'Connor, which he later revised on the grounds that it sounded implausible, and so it a good example of how interpreters find themselves on shifting sands. At one point Murphy-O'Connor argued that the Jews would have been accustomed to the idea that a woman had no authority of her own. According to Josephus, "[t]he woman, says the Law, is in all things inferior to the man. Let her accordingly be submissive, not for her humiliation, but that she may be directed; for the authority has been given by God to the man (*Ag. Ap.* 2.24 §201)." Paul, however, was overturning this law, by giving women full authority to act as they were doing, which would have quite naturally caused some consternation in the angelic world, accustomed as they were to the order of things. Women, therefore, needed to wear their hair plaited around the head as a wrapper (περιβόλαιον) in order to "convey their new status to the angels who watched for breaches of the Law. The guardians of an outmoded tradition had to be shown that things had changed."[28] In a later edition, he rescinds this view on the grounds that he now believes the reference to "angels" to refer to human messengers, although even this particular view of the angels as humans is not a well-attested reading.[29]

The second reading is from T. W. Martin who I will let speak for himself.

> The problem with Paul's argument from nature for the veiling of women in public worship in 1 Cor 11:13–15 arises not from Paul's convoluted logic or flawed argumentation but from the philological confusion of modern interpreters who fail to understand the ancient physiological conception of hair (κόμη) and confuse a testicle (περιβόλαιον) with a head covering. Hippocratic authors hold that long feminine hair assists the uterus in drawing semen

forbidden tree' (Cul. fem. 1.1, cf. 1 Tim. 2:14). Paul's veiling directives suggest a similar preoccupation with boundaries. That this is expressed in terms of the metaphysically secondary place of woman vis-à-vis man indicates that his rationale is analogous to his contemporaries. Women, as metaphysically secondary, are 'not quite men'; hence, they require a veil to ameliorate the risk that they cannot help but present." *Image and Glory*, 126.

28. Murphy-O'Connor, *Keys*, 155.

29. Ibid., 158.

upward and inward, while masculine testicles, which are connected to the brain where semen is stored by two channels, facilitate the drawing of semen downward and outward. Paul's argument contrasts long hair in woman with testicles in men and states that appropriate to her nature a woman is not given an external testicle but rather hair instead. The long, hollow hair on a woman's head is her glory because it enhances her female nature, which is to draw in and retain semen. Informed by the Jewish tradition, which strictly forbade display of genitalia when engaged in God's service, Paul instructs women in the service of God to cover their hair since it is part of the female genitalia.[30]

That this argument is even considered seriously enough to warrant refutation is bemusing to say the least.

Because of the Angels

On the knotty question of the angels, on whose account these head coverings must be worn, we continue to encounter disputes and contradictions. Are these guardian angels, visiting human messengers, evil angels, or fallen angels whose lusts must not be inflamed by the provocative bareheaded women? There is no clear answer here, although as with the rest of the difficult texts, that does not prevent commentators offering what they see as a plausible reading. Payne writes, "It ought to be embarrassing enough for a woman to be seen by others in the church with her hair let down, but knowing she is being observed by God's holy angels should be reason enough for even the most foolhardy woman to restrain her urge to let her hair down. Consequently, Paul writes that a woman ought to have control over her head on account of the angels' presence in worship."[31]

It seems clear that we have to admit that the nature of the angels for whom we must veil remains a mystery, although why any of those angels would, in our own time, no longer need to be protected from the shame of an unveiled woman is not something that most commentators tackle. This is only avoided if we understand the angels to be visiting human messengers, but there is no real textual support for this. I would suggest, however, if we take this to support head coverings for women as a Pauline apostolic ruling—on account of the angels—it must be presumed that angels are not

30. Abstract from Martin, "Paul's Argument from Nature," 75.

31. Payne, *Man and Woman,* 186.

subject to the vagaries of cultural trends, and that if offense was caused then, it must still be the case now.

Even though this text is obscure, the point should be noted. Paul endorses his creation-based rationale for head coverings with a cosmological reference. If head coverings or hairstyle reflect something of the order of creation and the cosmos, then who are we to abolish or adapt them? Most scholars are reluctant to posit a universal ruling for all women and to assert that this should be respected today in contemporary churches, although not all. It is still possible to find scholars and churchmen arguing that the practice of head coverings is an apostolic tradition that cannot be ignored even in the present day.[32] The latter position is more faithful to the text if we believe this to be Paul's view.

Verses 11–16: A Qualification or a Contradiction?

11 πλὴν οὔτε γυνὴ χωρὶς ἀνδρὸς οὔτε ἀνὴρ χωρὶς γυναικὸς ἐν κυρίῳ·

11 Nevertheless, in the Lord woman is not independent of man, neither is man independent of woman.

Before we leave the traditional readings, we must note the apparent shift that occurs in verse 11, which adds to the confusion. It has been noted by many scholars that the word πλὴν (nevertheless) first is adversative and second is used "to break off a discussion and to emphasize what is important."[33] Importantly, it is for this reason that Murphy-O'Connor and others make an exegetical decision to *prioritize* Paul's reciprocal picture of man and woman articulated in verses 11–16 over his patriarchal argument in verses 2–10. However, as we have seen, others are not so sure about claiming that Paul's "in Christ" or "in the Lord" theology of man and woman supersedes his creation theology, and prefer to hold the two in tension. Some still hold to the priority of Paul's creation theology in the first section. Despite Paul's claims in Galatians 3:28, C. K. Barrett goes so far as to say that "the oneness of male and female in Christ (Gal. iii.28) does not obliterate the distinction given in creation."[34] Barrett argues that the

---

32. See, for example, Terry, "'No Such Custom'"; The Head Covering Movement: 1 Corinthians 11 for Today http://www.headcoveringmovement.com/.

33. Murphy-O'Connor, *Keys*, 131.

34. Barrett, *A Commentary*, 251.

creation ordinances, extrapolated as they are in 1 Corinthians 11:3–10 (in a somewhat dubious fashion, as we have noted), may not be superseded by the new existence in Christ and the Spirit.

The initial difficulty for an interpreter of this passage arises over whether we perceive the two views as incompatible in the first place. If we perceive any tension at all, then we must either find a way of reconciling two opposing views, or we must make a decision about whether we allow one section to take precedence over another in terms of our view of man's relation to woman. A further problem with this shift at verse 11 is that it might appear that Paul is simply double-minded, illogical, contradictory, or vacillating, trying to please two parties at once.

Having surveyed different perspectives it is clear that there are multiple problems with these two sections juxtaposed with one another. Not only do they express radically different views of men and women, but they are predicated on very different readings of Genesis. In addition to this, we have to reconcile the first section with other passages in Paul, most specifically Galatians 3:28. I will discuss this in more detail below, but the following is an example of how 1 Corinthians 11:2–16 is read in contrast to Galatians 3:28. Murphy-O'Connor understands Galatians 3:28 as what might be described as a text that accords equality and mutuality to man and woman, but nevertheless believes that in 1 Corinthians Paul allowed pragmatic concerns of cultural appearances to override his theological principles.

> Paul denied the practical application of his principle of equality in situations where he saw its application was in danger of becoming a major distraction from the central concerns of Christian life, or where it was likely to prove an obstacle to the credibility of the church. These reasons carried greater weight with him than they possibly do with us because of his eschatological expectation, and because of his extremely pragmatic concern for the success of his mission.[35]

Whether we see these two sections juxtaposed as evidence of Paul's pragmatism, his muddleheadedness, his latent misogyny, or the gentle patriarchy he is unable to relinquish, we still have to find some way of reconciling two different accounts of the relations of men to women, men and women to Christ, and men and women and Christ to God. I will explore this further in the second section.

35. Murphy-O'Connor, *Keys*, 133.

An Apostolic Ruling?

16 εἰ δέ τις δοκεῖ φιλόνεικος εἶναι, ἡμεῖς τοιαύτην συνήθειαν οὐκ ἔχομεν, οὐδὲ αἱ ἐκκλησίαι τοῦ θεοῦ.

16 If anyone is disposed to be contentious/divisive—we have no such custom, nor do the churches of God.

Regardless of whether we choose to read this passage in relation to head coverings or hairstyles, if we believe this to be the voice of Paul, one of the important questions for the application of this passage is how adamant Paul is that this should be implemented, and whether we are going to read it as an apostolic ruling for all churches everywhere, or whether we will consign this particular injunction to a culturally specific context that is no longer binding on the church today. It is generally acknowledged that "no other practice" (NIV) is a bad translation of τοιαύτην συνήθειαν οὐκ, which should instead be translated "no such custom," as in the NRSV cited above. The latter is much more assertive than the former, which yields a softer reading. Benjamin Edsall writes: "The majority of scholars interpret this to mean 'we *recognize* no *other* practice,' though this is not what the statement says. In fact, it is the logical opposite. Rather than 'we have no other practice,' Paul states 'we do *not* have *that* practice.'"[36] On the question of the use of the word "contentious" or "divisive" most commentators agree that Paul is expressing a severe warning to those who would disagree with him. Barrett makes the point that contentiousness does not simply indicate someone who might disagree, but is a divisive and destructive characteristic of philosophers and therefore not at all a Christian virtue. So "anyone who wishes to argue against Paul's view on this matter should remember that he is putting himself in a minority of one."[37] Barrett's view on the uncompromising nature of Paul's injunction is well supported as we will see below, but why would Paul be quite so adamant about this? Whichever view we adopt, we must be willing to defend the fact that Paul sees the particular transgression as so serious that he wishes to enforce his ruling in all his churches. I believe I have demonstrated that in Paul's eyes this is a transgression of an egregious nature and not a minor peccadillo. I also believe that the text is clear that head coverings/hairstyles are a reflection of a God-given order in creation. If this is true, then we should be taking Paul's views more seriously

36. Edsall, "Greco-Roman Costume," 141–42.
37. Barrett, *A Commentary*, 257–58.

today, and if we are sure that he is committed to head coverings for women, then we should consider implementing this practice in our churches.

The Problems: A Summary

Let us note some of the problems thus far.

a. We face the difficulty of making a decision between "head covering" and "hair length." This centres on the Greek κατὰ κεφαλῆς in verse 4 meaning "having down on the head" or "having down from the head." Scholars are divided as to which it is.

b. We are unsure what exactly is the reason for the shame. Despite an insistence by many scholars that Paul is drawing his concepts of shame and honor in relation to head coverings or hairstyles from the culture around him, this is decisively undermined by those who admit that we cannot, in fact, make any assertions as to what exactly *was* shameful or honoring in terms of attire.

c. In relation to (b) we are also unsure as to the *source* of the shame that men and women are bringing upon themselves. There is a clear link in Paul's mind between the shame, the physical head, and the metaphysical spiritual head. We are unable to establish precisely what that link is, but from verse 7 we should deduce that it is related to his theology of glory, as reflected and symbolized by man and woman. Although this is explained in terms of "difference" or differentiation by a few scholars, there are others who interpret this in straightforwardly subordinationist terms. Because the behavior of men and women shames their metaphorical heads and not their own heads, it is very difficult to avoid the reading that men are not to be shamed either by obscuring their own glory (the image of God/Christ) or by being demeaned by the women's behavior, and that women are not to be shamed either by acting above their station, rejecting an outward sign of authority, or by demonstrating that they are prostitutes. There is a fundamental inequality between the two "sources" of shame.

d. Paul's creation theology in verses 7–9 is incompatible with the accounts in Genesis and with his own "in the Lord" theology, which he later refers to.

e. We do not know whether Paul is referring to all men and all women or husbands and wives.

f. We are dependent on historical reconstructions of the situation in Corinth that are highly speculative.

g. We do not know what the problem with the angels is.

h. We have to explain the relationship of verses 2–10 to verses 11–16, which together seem to generate contradictions or inconsistencies.

i. We do not know why Paul is so adamant that these practices should be implemented in all his churches.

Some Unavoidable Conclusions

Traditional readings of 1 Corinthians 11:2–16 yield a number of unavoidable conclusions. If we follow the hairstyle reading, we have to accept the fact that Paul was most concerned with the idea that men might be seen to be homosexual and that women might appear either promiscuous, defiant, and sexually immoral with long hair worn down, or as lesbians with short hair. We also have to accept, moreover, that hairstyles carried with them these particular and, at the same time, universal signifiers, for this was to be a ruling for *all* the churches. This argument is very difficult to prove given the range of cultural mores that operated at the time in a multicultural city such as Corinth, and further afield in the other churches under Paul's jurisdiction. Moreover, if we do accept this reading of the cultural mores in respect of hairstyles, we then have to argue that Paul, as a Jew who would have been accustomed to the idea that a man might have long hair (in view of a custom such as the Nazirite vow), made a decision to introduce a universal and new practice on account of how things might appear, i.e., that men should always wear their hair short, and women should always wear their hair up. A further complication with this argument arises when we remember that Paul did not cut his hair while in Corinth (as we know from Acts 18), which means he himself would have had long hair. As normal hair grows at a rate of half an inch a month, eighteen months of growth would have added nine inches to Paul's hair. What is he doing then saying that long hair is a disgrace on a man? It should also be noted that there are a large number of biblical scholars who reject this reading and agree with Witherington that there is no doubt the issue is head coverings.

If we follow the head coverings translation, we have to accept that Paul is introducing two rulings with respect to head coverings: one for men in ruling that they should not wear head coverings, and one for women—that they should. It should also be noted that for some ethnic groups in Corinth, these would be innovations. Whereas the ruling for women to cover would probably have been in line with Jewish and/or Roman custom, as Barrett and others point out, Paul's instruction that the men should be bareheaded in worship is definitely contrary to Jewish custom.[38] For Paul, himself a Jew, to have argued so strongly from nature for a custom that Jews did not follow is extraordinary. If, in view of the problems attending the cultural argument, we wish to avoid rooting "Paul's" argument in cultural considerations we are left with the hierarchical theological reading of creation offered in 1 Corinthians 11:3–9. This, however, is also far from simple. First, Paul himself goes on to contradict this reading in verses 11–16. These later verses actually support an egalitarian reading of the creation narrative, except that irrevocable damage is done to egalitarianism once we concede that Paul is most certainly advocating head coverings for women. It is very difficult to argue that this is simply a question of honor and shame shared by the sexes, based on the nature of men and women in creation. It is most likely that a head covering is a sign of subjection and inferiority of women to men. Conversely, the lack of head coverings for men is a sign of superiority, and prevents their demeaning themselves before God and women. Neither must be shamed in front of God, one another, or the angels, but the significance of the shame for either sex is radically different. Moreover, we must also concede that Paul was expecting this practice to be implemented in *all* the churches, because he is making it clear that there is no other custom anymore, and that if the Corinthians refuse to implement this practice then they will find that they are completely isolated among the churches.

We are confused both in the academic world and in the church. There is absolutely no consensus as to the real rationale as to why Paul would really want women to be veiled in worship. Is it theological or cultural? Is it a sign of authority or inferiority? Why should women veil to pray and prophesy at all? How do we read this in conjunction with 1 Corinthians 14:33–36, where women are told not speak, but to remain silent? How do we square Paul's ruling here with his theology of a new humanity in Christ? How does this view of men and women/husbands and wives align with the equality and mutuality in relations of men and women presented in

38. Ibid., 247.

1 Corinthians 7? If we are to take the whole passage as a representation of Paul's own views on the matter then it appears to be impossible to expunge subordinationism and inequality from this passage or to avoid the conclusion that Paul is making a universal ruling that should be binding on us today. It also seems impossible to cover up the fact that Paul speaks with two voices when it comes to the relation of men and women before God. Finally, since it is impossible, on the basis of traditional readings, to argue against the fact that Paul makes a link between dressings for the head and eternal spiritual truths, one would expect this passage to remain binding upon the church. Of course, very few churches do observe the instructions apparently issued in this passage, yet I have not come across an adequate account of why we are now at liberty to ignore this ruling altogether. At this point it seems evident that we have to admit at least one or more of the following options: (a) Paul is committed to the subordination of women to men in some form and believes this should be reflected by what we wear on our heads, (b) he is not a very good thinker and is prone to confusion, (c) the contemporary church has failed to observe Paul's clear and universally binding injunction. Because, in my view, none of these does justice to the text itself or to Paul's theology as presented throughout his letters, we will now turn to a possible alternative reading.

THREE

A Rhetorical Reading Revisited

Introduction

In 1987, Thomas Shoemaker suggested that the inconsistencies and problems so apparent in Paul's argument in 1 Corinthians 11:2–16 could largely be resolved by a rhetorical reading of the passage. Shoemaker, in a short and underdeveloped article, put forward the argument that in 1 Corinthians 11:2–10, Paul is representing a misguided Corinthian perspective on the necessity of head coverings for women, which he then goes on to refute in 1 Corinthians 11:11–16. He writes: "To the faction that would have women submit to veiling, Paul says no—their liberty (in Christ Jesus) is not to be seized from them. His response is based on the interrelationship between man and woman, on man's dependence on woman for birth, on nature's gift of a veil of hair, and lastly on the fact that no one else, anywhere in the churches of God, demands such submission to a sexual hierarchy."[1]

He goes on to add:

> It may never be possible to solve all the questions that now confront the church about this passage. But Paul should not so quickly be awarded a place of honor among those who would oppose egalitarian practice both inside and outside the church walls. There are too many plaguing problems surrounding the traditional interpretation of this passage for it to be so easily assumed. Paul the theologian of baptismal equality, Paul the pastor of reconciliation, and Paul the master rhetorician all seem to say the opposite.[2]

1. Shoemaker, "Unveiling of Equality," 63.
2. Ibid., 63.

As far as I am aware, there are two other commentators who have argued along these lines in some way, attempting to demonstrate that the first section contains elements of the Corinthians' thought and the second section of the passage contains Paul's.[3] Although this possibility has not yet been explored satisfactorily, the principle that Paul may be employing a form of rhetoric in which he cites his opponents in order to argue against head coverings has either been dismissed or largely ignored. In this chapter, I will outline the plausibility of a rhetorical argument, and the weaknesses of the claims that the call for the covering and the silencing of women in 1 Corinthians comes from Paul.

Reasons for Exploring a Rhetorical Argument

First, as we have noted, there is a spectacular array of contradictory commentary on this passage in scholarly circles. The sheer level of confusion that this text gives rise to should cause us to wonder if we have yet found an adequate explanation. Related to this is the fact that if there are clear injunctions in 1 Corinthians against women praying bareheaded or speaking up in church, these injunctions are consistently and comprehensively ignored by the majority of churches in the world. This is an indication that we do not take these passages seriously. Second, the rhetorical reading has not yet been adequately refuted; it is difficult to find any really robust refutation of it. Lakey rejects any such rhetorical reading on the grounds that there is nowhere else that Paul quotes the Corinthians at such length, therefore, he cannot be doing so here.[4] I appreciate that, thus far, the "slogans" that have been identified as Corinthian within Paul's letters are not very long.[5] There is general agreement that the following verses are Corinthian slogans

3. See Padgett, *As Christ Submits to the Church*; Vadakkedom, "The Letter of Corinthians to Paul the Apostle."

4. With reference to Padgett's argument, Lakey writes, "However, since most of Paul's other citations of the Corinthians take the form of sentences or clauses, not entire paragraphs, there is no evidence to suggest that Paul cites his interlocutors as extensively as Padgett proposes." *Image and Glory*, 100.

5. Thiselton believes that the use of expanded rhetorical repetition "seems to provide a decisive objection to Alan Padgett's view that vv. 4–7 represent a Corinthian statement which Paul rejects. When Paul cites a slogan from Corinth . . . he does so succinctly." *The First Epistle*, 833. Fee admits that it is an attractive proposal, but demurs that this does not seem to deal adequately "with Paul's relationship with the church as a whole . . . or with the *structure* of the argument in particular (concern over men's dress does not seem to be in purview)." *First Epistle*, 497n.19.

thereby demonstrating that in every other instance, Paul only uses one or two phrases: 6:12, 13; 7:1; 8:1, 8:4; 10:23; 15:12. However, this refutation is not particularly decisive. The idea that "Paul does not quote at length here because he does not do this anywhere else in 1 Corinthians" is not in itself a definitive objection. Currently scholars are only agreed on certain short phrases as Corinthian slogans. However, the fact that he does include Corinthian phrases in this letter (albeit short ones), rather than precluding the possibility of a longer citation, could equally be an indicator that there are more references to Corinthian thought than we have previously noticed. Moreover, if we can show that it is more than likely that Paul cites longer phrases in his method of argumentation in more than one place in 1 Corinthians 11–14, as I shall endeavor to do, then this objection becomes invalid.

Third, the historical reconstructions that support the traditional view are not particularly convincing. We find ourselves being told that it is easy to "imagine" this or that. These are highly subjective claims. Is it really easier to imagine Christian women in first-century Corinth behaving in the way proposed than it is to imagine a church in first-century Graeco-Roman culture in which a group of men are behaving in a domineering way towards the women, forcing them to wear a sign on their heads that protects them from some form of imagined infringement? I have not yet found any commentator who does not acknowledge that this culture had what Payne describes as a "broadly misogynist streak." Women were inferior to men. Poor women were doubly inferior. They were conditioned that way, and no doubt many women believed it to be truly the case.[6] Bristow documents the widespread belief in the inferiority of women in Graeco-Roman culture stemming from the ancients. In relation to Aristotle, he writes:

> He formalized the practice of sexual discrimination and offered learned authority to the belief in sexual inequality. Centuries later,

6. Payne notes the prevalence of misogynist writings and the generally accepted view that women were inferior to men, both by virtue of being perceived to have been created inferior, and by virtue of their inherent lack of gifts and virtue. He cites examples from Euripides (c.479–406 BC), Plato (c.437–347 BC), Aristotle (384–322 BC), Menander (c.343–291 BC), Democritus, Pseudo-Lucian (post-second century AD), and Plutarch (c.46–120 AD) cataloguing quotes depicting women as inferior, weaker, temptresses, evil, misfits, the property of man, and even "the female as a deformed male" (Aristotle, *Gen. an.* 737a and 775a). The general trend is summed up by Plato, "Do you know, then, of anything practiced by mankind in which the masculine sex does not surpass the female on all these points? . . . [The] one sex is far surpassed by the other in everything, one may say . . . the woman is weaker than the man" (*Resp.* 5.455c-e), cited in *Man and Woman*, 32–34.

church leaders who themselves were a product of Greek culture and education interpreted Paul's writings from the perspective of Aristotelian philosophy, even to the point of assuming that when Paul wrote of the husband being head of the wife, he was simply restating Aristotle's analogy of the husband being to his wife like one's soul to one's body.[7]

On the reception of Paul's teaching by the Gentiles, he notes that the Gentiles whom Paul was evangelizing and seeking to bring to faith in Jesus Christ "brought with them the Greek notions of female inferiority, espoused the same interpretations of the Old Testament as those of the Hellenized Jews, and used Paul's writings to give authority to the same philosophical viewpoint that Paul opposed."[8]

Either we have to imagine that these women who have been brought up in this culture have become completely uncontrolled and uncontrollable, or that the entire church (men and women) had abandoned Paul's teaching and practices on gender differentiation in some way. Why is this any easier to imagine in first-century Corinth than to imagine that there might have been a group of powerful and spiritually gifted men, who in Paul's absence implemented teaching and practices that reinforced a particular hierarchical view of men and women based on a creation theology of derivation? What is easier to imagine than converts reverting to their cultural norms and pre-Christian world views? If this were to be the case, why would Paul not want to liberate women (a) from bad theology in relation to their status in Christ and (b) from an oppressive practice?

The fourth reason pertains to Paul's view of shame and honor in relation to what we understand of a Corinthian view of shame and honor. The traditional view of this passage rests on the centrality and governing nature of the shame/honor motif. It is intriguing in the light of the rest of the letter that no one questions the fundamental inconsistency in claiming that the same person who wrote 1 Corinthians 1 and 2, 1 Corinthians 4, and 1 Corinthians 15 should take such a view on the necessity of sheltering one another from shame and dishonor in public worship in 1 Corinthians 11. This is Paul who mockingly says to the Corinthians, "We are fools for Christ, but you are so wise in Christ! We are weak, but you are strong!" completing his taunt by reversing the order and placing the Corinthians first, thus driving home his point about the difference between them and

7. Bristow, *What Paul*, 6–7.
8. Ibid., 27–28.

69

the true apostles. "You are honored," he declaims, but "we are dishonored!" Apostleship for Paul is *marked* by public dishonor and disgrace. "For I think that God has exhibited us apostles as last of all, as though sentenced to death, because we have become a spectacle to the world, to angels and to mortals" (1 Cor 4:9) or "For it seems to me that God has put us apostles on display at the end of the procession, like men condemned to die in the arena. We have been made a spectacle to the whole universe, to angels as well as men" (NIV). The angels are indeed watching, and what they see is the true apostles vilified and shamed in the public arena. Following Christ for Paul means being identified as the lowest of the low, the scum of the earth, the scrapings from the bottom of a shoe (1 Cor 4:8–13). It is hard to do justice to Paul's descriptions of himself and his apostleship in the extreme language that he uses. Paul claims that God chooses the foolish, the lowly, the weak, and the despised *in order to shame* the wise, the strong, and the boastful (1 Cor 1:20–31). We are not yet in possession of our heavenly glorious bodies. Our bodies are currently sown in dishonor, to be raised in glory at the final resurrection (1 Cor 15:43). The glory that we will display is yet to come. We know that Paul believed the Corinthians to be arrogant and self-seeking. His magisterial proclamation on the nature of true Christlike love in chapter 13 bears witness to the fact that he is addressing a fundamental ethical flaw within the Corinthian church concerning their treatment of one another. Is it possible that the men, in their arrogance and obsession with status, were requiring a sign of public honor to be instantiated in head coverings for women, and that married women should defer to their husbands in public worship, rather than speaking out and questioning what was happening?

Witherington brings out the importance of shame and honor within the Corinthian culture. "The Corinthian people thus lived with an honor-shame cultural orientation, where public recognition was often more important than facts. . . . In such a culture a person's sense of worth is based on recognition by others of one's accomplishments."[9] He notes this with a view to explaining why Paul on the one hand justifies his own position and, on the other, issues a scathing critique of their "obsessive concern to win reputation and status in the eyes of others." "In a city where social climbing was a major preoccupation, Paul's deliberate stepping down in apparent

9. Witherington, *Conflict and Community*, 21.

status would have been seen by many as disturbing, disgusting, and even provocative."[10]

Thiselton notes the same theme, bringing out Paul's own identification with the crucified Christ. "Christ's rejection as one 'dishonored' or 'disgraced' by the shame of the cross colors Paul's language in 4:8–13."[11] When Paul refers to a spectacle, he would have been referring to prisoners, criminals, or professional gladiators processing into the gladiatorial ring. "Paul perceives his apostolic labors as a cosmic spectacle, which, if they are evaluated by Corinthian criteria, seem to be a spectacle of struggle, failure, and disgrace."[12] What light does this shed on Paul's putative theology of shame and honor, glory, inferiority, and superiority in chapter 11? First, even if Paul did actually think that man alone was the image and glory of God, this would in no way exonerate "man" from having to situate himself in a crucified position along with Christ. Equally, there is no possible way that a woman could avoid being identified with the crucified Christ, along with the men, and with Paul. Man, woman, and Christ all occupy Christ's position—which is what? According to Paul, in the world's eyes, it is the lowest of the low. The glory is yet to come. Against the Corinthians, Paul is arguing that Christ—and therefore Paul also—takes the lower part. In Christ, Paul aligns himself with the shamed, the dishonored, the disgraced. Paul identifies with Christ, and in doing so, is identified with what in Roman society would have been the sinful woman's (not necessarily the wealthy woman's) and the slave's position. Paul as apostle aligns himself with the feminine and the slaves.

However, it is not just that the crucified Christ is the dishonored one. Jesus in his life was shamed and dishonored in public by women. Paul's master, the one whom he had encountered and whom he followed slavishly, was the one who had been approached by a sinful, shameful, and dishonorable woman. She disgraced him in public by uncovering his feet, anointing them with oil, weeping over him, and then wiping his feet *with her hair*.[13] The men were outraged, not only by her, but by Jesus' acceptance of her lavish and disgraceful gesture. Who did she think she was and what was Jesus doing allowing this breach of cultural codes? What did Jesus mean by

10. Ibid., 21.

11. Thiselton, *The First Epistle*, 367.

12. Ibid., 360.

13. The connection between 1 Cor 11 and John 12:1–8 was first brought to my attention by Joel Mennie.

allowing her to do this? All four Gospel writers tell this story in some form or another. Matthew, however, records an astonishing statement. Jesus rebuked his critics. "Truly I tell you, wherever this good news is proclaimed in the whole world, what she has done will be told, in remembrance of her" (Matt 26:6–13; Mark 14:3–9; Luke 7:36–47; John 12:1–8). The story is told, not in memory of the Savior, but in memory of *her*. Her disgraceful act is the very means by which she is now honored.

Finally, we should locate Paul's teaching in chapters 11 and 14 (the latter of which we will come to in more detail below) on the covering and silencing of women in worship in his wider theology of men and women and marriage. It is my contention that we have not yet explored the implications of both Galatians 3:28 and 1 Corinthians 7:1–7 in relation to these passages, and how seriously they call into question both the establishment of boundaries between men and women in worship, and the silencing of women in the gathered assembly. What precisely Paul means by declaring that there is now "neither Jew nor Gentile, slave nor free, male nor female" is much debated, but both Campbell's contribution on Jew and Gentile relations in Christ, and N. T. Wright's work on Philemon are pertinent here. If we understand what Paul is saying with reference to the first two pairings, then this will help us to understand what he might mean by including men and women in this statement in Galatians.

In relation to Jew and Gentile, Campbell argues that Paul presents an eschatological gospel in which "Jewish and non-Jewish life-styles and peoples has been subsumed in the broader supersession of all created human existence, hence the apparently redundant claims concerning the abolition of class and gender actually participate significantly in his argument by indicating the cosmic sweep of this assertion. . . . This point is especially clear if Paul alludes to Gen. 1:27 in v. 28a. That textual echo would suggest that Paul's framework is creational (which is to say that the symmetrical counterpoint to Christ's work for Paul is Adam; another plausible suggestion surely)."[14] Here Campbell outlines the crucial place of baptism in creating a new form of human relations where the Christian's status of "sonship" takes precedence over the normal categories of differentiation within society, especially with regard to superior/inferior relations.

> Paul seems to be deploying spatial categories consistently in order
> to speak of categories of existence or being and their transforma-
> tion in relation to the events of Easter. (The Galatians are said, in

14. Campbell, *The Quest*, 101–2.

the space of three verses, to be "in Christ" [and this twice], to be clothed "in" Christ, and to be immersed "into" Christ.) He interprets this to mean that the Galatian Christians, irrespective of their previous positioning within the potentially diverse subcategories of present society, have been shifted into a mutually exclusive category of uniform sonship in Christ that displaces their previous existence, whatever it was—a dramatic set of claims! [15]

He adds that this shift is "best symbolized in certain respects by the ritual of baptism."[16]

In a similar vein, N. T. Wright explores the impact of Paul's "in Christ" theology to the categories of slave and free that emerges in his letter to Philemon. Wright argues that the main theme of this little letter is "reconciliation" between two men who are now brought into a familial relationship of unity, both through and in the Messiah, and driven by the Spirit. Onesimus is Paul's beloved son and therefore is Philemon's beloved brother.[17] "The whole letter is both an expression of, and an exhortation to, the central Pauline theme of *koinonia*, 'fellowship' or 'partnership'—a word with multiple resonances."[18] Crucially, however, he is arguing that as Onesimus and Philemon are now beloved brothers; the social categories are no longer left intact. "Those who have read this letter without seeing the profound, and profoundly revolutionary, theology it contains should ponder the social and cultural earthquake which Paul is attempting to precipitate—or rather, which he believes has already been precipitated by God's action in the Messiah."[19] Wright emphasizes the unity of the Jew and Gentile in the Messiah (the main point of Galatians), that goes across traditional boundaries, but crucially, that has concrete and visible ramifications for society. This is not some other-worldly vision that Paul is looking forward to at some point in the future, but a concrete reality for the people of God who are now "in Christ."

Although Wright mentions the category of men and women, he does not make anything of the implications of Paul's inclusion of male and female in this regard. This begs the question, however, of what this messianic unity across traditional boundaries might look like in concrete terms in the body

15. Ibid., 99–100.

16. Ibid., 100.

17. Wright, *Paul*, 9.

18. Ibid., 11.

19. Ibid., 9.

of Christ. According to Campbell and Wright, we could claim that men and women, along with Jew and Gentile, and slave and free, are now "sons" and "coheirs" with Christ—brothers and sisters. Familial categories supersede traditional boundaries. As Wright notes, "The heart of it all, as already suggested, is *koinonia*, a 'partnership' or 'fellowship' which is not static, but which enables the community of those who believe to grow together into a unity across the traditional divisions of the human race."[20] The authority that Paul has is precisely because he is "a prisoner of the Messiah, Jesus . . . and it is the Messiah's people, bringing together Jew and Greek, slave and free, male and female, that are designated corporately as *Christos*."[21]

Wright emphasizes Paul's "in Christ" theology; however, in this little letter, Paul uses the phrase ἐν κυρίῳ (in the Lord) in verse 16 as the descriptor for Philemon's new relationship with Onesimus, and as a rationale for Philemon to now view him in a different light. Onesimus and Philemon are beloved brothers "in the Lord." In the same letter, Paul describes Apphia as his "sister." This is directly relevant to 1 Corinthians. In 1:11, men and women are also described by Paul as being ἐν κυρίῳ, and this in connection with the fact that he is emphasizing their mutual interdependence and provenance. The idea that we are united in Christ through baptism and the Spirit is, of course, a key theme of this letter (1 Cor 12:13). Some note that in contrast to Galatians 3:28 Paul omits the categories of male and female in this verse and wonder whether Paul is deliberately omitting male and female to make a point. I would argue that he does not need to reiterate what he has so strongly claimed already in 1 Corinthians 11:11.

Unity in the Community

Paul is writing to them specifically to combat the division that is plaguing the community. What emerges in the letter, however, is Paul's clear expectation that this familial unity will have concrete and visible manifestations in their common life together and particularly in worship, which includes the use of spiritual gifts and the celebration of the Lord's Supper. In these two areas, the Corinthians are woefully inadequate. Paul addresses his letter to a group whose meetings do more harm than good (11:17) because they are riven with divisions and tainted by the bad behavior of those who are lording it over others, the rich and privileged depriving the poor. "Or do you

20. Ibid., 16.
21. Ibid., 21.

show contempt for the church of God and humiliate those who have nothing?" (11:22). Paul enjoins them to care for one another, especially those in need, "so then, my brothers and sisters, when you come together to eat, wait for one another" (11:33). The strong are to care for the weak, but also to give them greater honor. "[O]n the contrary, those parts of the body that seem to be weaker are indispensable, and the parts that we think are less honorable we clothe with greater honor. But God has so arranged the body, giving the greater honor to the inferior member, that there may be no dissension within the body, but the members may have the same care for one another. If one member suffers, all suffer together with it; if one member is honored, all rejoice together with it . . ." (12:22–25).

There is a case to be made that "egalitarianism" is an inappropriate concept to read into Paul. Nevertheless, what are the implications of Paul's "in Christ" theology, that we are *all* designated corporately as *Christos*? What does it mean that Paul was the opponent of circumcision for Gentile Christ-believers and the reconciler of the slave and the free into a newfound brotherhood? This will give us a key to understanding his vision for men and women as brothers and sisters. Tom O'Loughlin in a discussion on the early Eucharist makes the point that 1 Corinthians 12 is a new picture of the universe and one in which the slave eats with the master.[22] This is a radically new order. One of the most powerful concrete manifestations of this new order is that Jew and Gentile, slave and free, male and female enjoy table fellowship together—with those who are traditionally inferior given the greater honor. The traditional boundaries have not only been erased, but redrawn in a radically new way. Notions of unclean and clean, superiority and inferiority, privilege and underprivilege are eradicated at the meal of remembrance, and those who are traditionally excluded or marginalized are now the privileged ones. Jesus' table was occupied with tax collectors and sinners, drunks, women, prostitutes, and slaves. He instructs his disciples to be those who take the lower position and Paul follows suit. As O'Loughlin notes, "the Eucharist breaks all social boundaries," "the table becomes the symbol of welcome."[23] In contrast to the Graeco-Roman table that is highly stratified, where the rich use the meal as an opportunity to display their largesse, the communion table is a new altar where worldly status is irrelevant, where those who have make way for those who have not, where outsiders are welcomed. The communion table is where Jew and Gentile,

22. O'Loughlin, "Why Study the Early Eucharist?"
23. Ibid.

slave and free, man and woman sit and eat as brothers and sisters. Barriers and boundaries come down in worship. Those who have traditionally been separated in the temple by Jewish law now find themselves not only worshipping together, but eating together as one. Grant Macaskill writes that Paul, in 1 Corinthians 11, is targeting the institutionalized humiliation of the "have-nots" (11:22).[24] "Paul reminds his readers that the very tradition of the Lord's Supper that has been handed down is of the divine purpose in Jesus's death that pronounces a verdict on the very social distinctions that they cherish and maintain."[25] His point is that Jesus' death proclaimed in the sacrament thoroughly contradicts the segregation of rich and poor practiced at Corinth. "Paul's principal concern in 1 Corinthians 11:17–34 is with a practice of the Supper that involves or exacerbates distinctions and divisions rather than unity."[26]

In addition to this, Paul's radical picture of marriage in 1 Corinthians 7:1–7 should also cause us to stop and think about his apparent silencing of married women. Any first-century male who declares that a wife has "authority over (ἐξουσιάζει) her husband's body" is making a truly radical claim about men and women in marriage. If this is indeed Paul's theology, then both the covering of women and the silencing of married women in the worship strikes a harshly discordant note. Those who argue that Paul's views are expressed in 1 Corinthians 11:3–10 must make a much stronger case for why Paul instigates practices that re-establish boundaries and divisions in worship between men and women. What does it mean to hold, on the one hand, to a creation theology of derivation which necessitates the covering of women, and on the other, to an "in the Lord" theology in which he argues that a woman's covering is her hair. It is a grave error to underestimate both the significance and implications of Paul's statement "in the Lord" and to miss the force with which this insight is delivered in verse 11. For all these reasons, we should at least explore the possibility that Paul's approach to how women should be treated "in the Lord" was far more radical than we might allow, and that he might actually have been concerned to release the women from a patriarchal and theologically flawed practice designed to keep women in their proper place. As I have noted before, the overwhelming evidence is that we must either accept that Paul invests a

24. Macaskill, *Union with Christ*, 209.
25. Ibid., 210.
26. Ibid., 208.

cultural practice with deep theological significance, or we must reimagine what he might be saying.

The Art of Rhetoric

There has been a growing interest in Paul's use of rhetoric in his letters, as well as an acknowledgement that Paul's letters are carefully crafted epistles designed in their argumentation to effect a response among his hearers. I propose, therefore, that we should revisit the idea of a rhetorical reading of this passage as an interpretative possibility, and I suggest that by doing so we will more effectively discern the content and consistency of Paul's overall message in 1 Corinthians, as well as demonstrating how this letter aligns with Pauline theology in general. I contend that most of the intractable problems faced in interpreting 1 Corinthians 11:2–16 only arise if we understand verses 2–10 to be expressing Paul's theology just as much as the views expressed in verses 11–16. In other words, if we continue to attempt to read verses 2–16 as a whole and as wholly representative of Paul's theology and practice, then Fee's points are apposite. Traditional readings of 1 Corinthians 11:2–16 (a) struggle to articulate the logic of the argument itself, (b) fail to reach a consensus on the meanings of certain words or phrases, (c) fail to explain adequately why Paul himself would introduce what could be viewed either as a Jewish pietistic practice or a Roman sign of decorum for all women in all churches, (d) do not give a satisfactory answer as to why Paul would simultaneously introduce an innovation for men regarding head coverings in worship, (e) are unable to reach a consensus either on the customs of the day, both in respect of the practices of the time and the signification of head coverings, and (f) attempt to explain away what should be viewed as apostolic rulings on the conduct of women in worship as cultural constructs or later interpolations which we are free to ignore. The results of the traditional readings are highly problematic. Not only is the level of disagreement among scholars unusually stark in relation to this passage, but these readings also force us into admitting inconsistencies in Paul's thought within this particular letter and between this letter and other key aspects of his theology expressed in other epistles.

An alternative way of reading this passage is that Paul has interwoven Corinthian ideas and phrases into verses 2–16, along with his own ideas, but as the Corinthians knew what they were doing and saying in the first place, they would have understood this section of the letter to be Paul's argument *against* head coverings for women. With this reading many of our intractable problems with the passage will be resolved. A rhetorical reading of the passage as a carefully crafted form of argumentation against the Corinthians' own views will yield five crucial results. First, it will go a long way to solving the exegetical problems inherent within the text, or what Fee calls the "logic" of the passage. We will cease to be forced to reconcile the logic of verses 2–10 with verses 11–16. As we have noted, this exercise clearly requires some explanatory contortions based on speculative suggestions as to Paul's state of mind, Paul's pragmatic missionary strategy, the customs of the day, and the self-styled disrespectful practices of the Corinthian church that Paul is purported to be addressing and correcting. Second, we will cease to have to explain Paul's theology of male and female where he appears to be conveying confusing messages. Third, it will resolve the question of having to accept that Paul might have ruled that all women everywhere, of whatever ethnic grouping, should conform to a Jewish or Roman practice of wearing a head covering in public worship and while praying and prophesying. It is still unclear why those who argue for this as the ruling of Paul believe that men and women should be released from these constraints today. Those who are shamed are not dishonored in the eyes of the surrounding culture, but because of the God-ordained relations one with another; presumably this still applies. The point here is not only that there are problems in relation to the practices supposed to have been universally implemented by Paul, but that Paul most certainly views head attire or hairstyles as theologically significant in relation to gender, shame, and honor. How do we apply this today? Fourth, when read in the context of the letter as a whole, it then makes sense of Paul's overall message in 1 Corinthians in which, I suggest, he is targeting practices implemented by the "spiritual" or spiritually gifted male leaders who have introduced a number of ungodly practices into the times of public worship, none of which Paul approves of. Fifth, it allows us to read 1 Corinthians as entirely consistent with Paul's theology of the body of Christ and the work of the Spirit, so central to all his thought.

An Alternative Scenario

As we have already noted, it is well nigh impossible to reconstruct an entirely accurate picture of the Corinthian church and milieu; however, there are significant clues in the text from which we can reconstruct certain possible scenarios. Witherington in his book *Conflict and Community* notes a number of factors that would support a reading of the text in which the troublesome group that Paul is addressing is made up of *men* and not women. In general, the problems in Corinth identified by Witherington are as follows:

a. partisan attachments to particular Christian teachers;

b. continuing adherence to particular cultural values, especially on the part of the wealthy, leading to lawsuits among fellow Christians;

c. unequal treatment of the Lord's table and dining in pagan temples;

d. hubris on the part of some who are using certain spiritual gifts in ways that do not build up the community;

e. disagreements regarding sexual conduct appropriate for Christians, both within and outside marriage;

f. disagreements over eschatological matters such as the resurrection and whether the present state of the believer involves reigning, glory, and the like.[27]

Witherington identifies a number of reasons why Paul would not be committed to a theological understanding of the inferiority of women. His strongest argument against the idea that Paul affirms a male human hierarchy in Christ is that he is clearly "quite comfortable talking about women as his co-workers, as fellow servants of God, and possibly even *apostoloi*." Phoebe was a *prostatis* or leader in Corinth's port city of Cenchreae and there is a warrant for claiming that Chloe was the leader of a house church[28] (Rom 16:1).

Although Witherington himself believes that Paul is addressing a problem with the women in chapter 11, he notes that, overall, Paul is generally addressing the men. In his view, "Paul's primary antagonists in Corinth were [probably] not women but well-to-do Gentile men." He goes on to add, "[f]urthermore, 1 Corinthians 5–6 and 8–10 certainly point to men as the source of trouble. . . . Even ch. 7, when studied closely, does not support the reconstruction of an ascetical pneumatic group of women in Corinth that Paul is particularly targeting."[29] What is interesting for my argument are some of his further observations.

---

27. Witherington, *Conflict and Community*, 74.

28. Ibid., 235.

29. Ibid., 232.

Perhaps some were urging the following of Roman practices in regard to headcoverings in worship while others were urging Jewish customs or possibly even the customs in some pagan mysteries, where women might worship without headcoverings and with their hair unbound. In a Roman city like Corinth it would not have seemed strange for women to have their heads covered during religious acts.[30]

It is not implausible that, if it was culturally acceptable for women to be covered during worship in a city like Corinth, the men in the church were continuing to force women to comply with a cultural practice that Paul had in fact released them from on the basis that they had a newfound freedom in Christ.

Witherington notes that the Romans were more careful than the Greeks in what they wore and "were more dominated by status and rules in their choice of garb when praying or sacrificing. Sometimes these rules were rigidly maintained; for example, the flamen dialis, a Roman sacerdotal official, was not allowed out of his house without a tight-fitting cap with a spike at the top. It appears that such headcoverings were worn in Roman contexts to demonstrate respect and subservience to the gods."[31] It is entirely plausible that with this cultural background the men of Corinth would have been loathe to release the women from the obligation to go without a head covering. Witherington goes on to note, correctly in my view, that Paul was about the "business of reforming his converts' social assumptions and conventions in the context of the Christian community."[32] He goes on to claim, "In this chapter, then, Paul is trying to reform both men and women in the Corinthian congregation who continue to take their cues for religious behavior from analogous practices in other religious settings in Corinth."[33] It is quite clear that this argument could just as well be applied to Paul's argument *against* head coverings, and in fact, with the cultural background that Witherington constructs, it is *more* likely in my view that the congregation would have complied with head coverings for women than that they would have been throwing them off.

This is further supported by Winter's speculation about what might have happened in the Corinthian church in Paul's absence. Winter believes

30. Ibid., 236.
31. Ibid., 234.
32. Ibid., 235.
33. Ibid., 239.

that the Corinthians had lost sight of Paul's teachings after he left Corinth, and had fallen prey to the influence of secular ethics or social conventions. "They may have crept into the church imperceptibly and grown with the passage of time."[34] His view is that Paul is addressing a specifically masculine culture of dominance, competitiveness, rivalry, and divisiveness that was more akin to the Roman culture of the day than to the Christlikeness in leadership that Paul had modeled for them. There were a group of men in the church behaving "like other men do" (3:3), i.e., like the secular Romans with one another, with jealousy, quarrelling, and rivalry. Fee believes that the anti-Pauline sentiment comes from a few who were infecting the whole (15:12; 4:18). Paul describes them variously as childish and immature, puffed up and arrogant, as sexually immoral, and as behaving selfishly at the Lord's Supper. The ones in control were probably the spiritually gifted, the natural leaders, the articulate, and the prophetic. In 1 Corinthians 1:5–7 Paul notes that they are not lacking in any spiritual gifts, and that they were enriched in Christ with all speech and all knowledge in every way. Moreover, they were clever with words.

Most commentators who take part in the process of "imagining" what might have been the case in Corinth when we attempt to piece together the text in conjunction with what we know of the culture. I have to admit that personally I find it easy to imagine a different scenario that I would describe in the following way: the Corinthian church was being dominated by a group of spiritually gifted and highly articulate teachers who were both overbearing and divisive men. Under their influential leadership, certain oppressive practices had been implemented, and other destructive and selfish practices had remained unchallenged. It was they who believed, among other things, and partially from a version of Paul's teaching in the first place, that men and women should display signs of their own status before God, one another, and the angels in worship. Because, according to Genesis 2, women were created second, the Corinthians were teaching that they have a secondary place in the creation order, deriving their glory not directly from Christ, but from man. For this reason, they needed to wear a sign of authority/subjection/honor on their "heads." As man is the glory of Christ, and Christ is the "head" of man, however, he must display this glory by remaining bareheaded. I imagine that these men could have been both powerful and forceful, pronouncing the "word of God," laying down the law, and arguing that if a woman was bareheaded this was tantamount

34. Winter, *After Paul*, 4.

to appearing before God as a prostitute and thus shaming the men, the angels, and God himself—she may as well appear shaven. They may even have articulated this in their letter to Paul. In short, the Corinthian men would have had a proclivity for conforming to worldly standards of shame and honor, and would have been forceful and gifted enough to enforce them. In the light of Witherington's observations regarding the Corinthian obsession with status, and the Roman, Greek, and Jewish culture into which Paul introduced the gospel of Christ, as well as the textual evidence for Paul's correctives to the men, this explanation is just as plausible—indeed, perhaps more plausible—than the wild women theory. In addition to this, reading the passage as an argument against head coverings has a substantial effect on the logic of the passage and the countless exegetical difficulties that we have noted.

A Proposal for an Alternative Reading

If we posit that Paul was utilizing a Greek rhetorical device in order to make the point to the Corinthian church that they should *not* force women to wear head coverings, we find that a number of the problems with the traditional readings disappear. First, the passage takes on its own logic, which I will go on to demonstrate. Second, the problematic translations of certain words cease to pose intractable problems, as they are part of the Corinthian argument that Paul is rehearsing back to them. Third, Paul's negation of head coverings for women, which he himself argues for in verses 11–16, is entirely consonant with his theology in the passage itself, in 1 Corinthians itself, and in other letters, most clearly spelled out in Galatians. Fourth, it makes sense of why Paul is telling them that there is no such custom (the wearing of head coverings for women) in any other church. Fifth, it accords with other passages in Corinthians where it is recognized that Paul is responding to the Corinthians' letter, repeating their argument to them, and then going on to refute it. Sixth, and finally, this reading accords with the view cited above that Paul is using this letter to address with some force certain ungodly practices that some in the church have implemented in his absence. We will deal with each of these in turn.

Campbell notes some characteristics of Greek philosophical rhetoric in relation to agonistic and diatribal argumentation, making the point that there is often an indirect form of argumentation employed rather than a "frontal polemical assault." This indirect approach is well documented, and is described in the following terms.

> Hence, good philosophers functioned as midwives, bringing truth to birth in their interlocutors from their own assumptions, teasing out a correct understanding by a process of cross-examination, *because the truth was already there*. (In particular, interlocutors could be confronted with the contradictions in their own positions and forced to abandon at least one half of such dilemmas, or they could be pressed to accept notions implicit within everyday analogies that they already affirmed, and so on.)[35]

Quoting Epictetus in *Upon the art of argumentation* (2.12.4–6), Campbell notes, "'the real guide, whenever he finds a person going astray, leads him back to the right road. . . . How did Socrates act? He used to force the man who was arguing with him to be his witness: . . . he used to make so clear the consequences which followed from the concepts, that absolutely everyone realized the contradiction involved and gave up the battle.'"[36] Diatribal discussion could be conducted in this indirect form, rendering the confrontation less offensive and directly polemical, while the author "still retains a high degree of control over that discussion." So Campbell writes, "An opposing construct is encoded by a diatribal discussion and then addressed before a text's audience. Particular people are therefore not named (or at least, not necessarily), and neither is the audience addressed aggressively, in a direct fashion. Moreover, even that construct is permitted to speak."[37] He goes on to add, "as often as not, that figure will be addressed and ultimately corrected in terms of his or her own assumptions. This technique is innate to the discourse's entire tradition, from its origins in the Socratic dialogue onward. So not only will a diatribal discourse's auditors be prompted to identify a figure who will ultimately be corrected, but they will expect that figure to receive instruction in relation to his or her own point of view, and so will either supply that point of view to the text—which is easy if the figure is a stereotype—or will be prompted explicitly by the text's encoding of that position."[38]

The idea that Paul reproduces "the position of other people which he then generally goes on to correct if not to criticize" is recognized in Paul's

35. Campbell, *Deliverance*, 536.
36. Ibid.
37. Ibid., 537.
38. Ibid.

writings.[39] Campbell writes, "It is worth noting that it is widely if not universally conceded that Paul behaves in essentially this fashion—quoting the positions of others, often unannounced—in the rest of his letters" and that there are "uncontested instances" of this in 1 Corinthians, namely 1:12; 3:4; 6:12–13; 7:1; 8:1; 4; 8; and 10:23.[40] He goes on to add possibly also 4:6b; 8:5a; 12:3; 15:12, 35. Campbell does not include 1 Corinthians 11 in his list. He does summarize however, in the following way: "In sum, it seems that Paul does quote texts from others when composing his letters, *and that he does not always signal those overtly with written cues . . ."*[41] (my italics).

As I noted at the beginning of the book, it could be that Paul is weaving his argument together by picking up some ideas and expressions from them but also including his own ideas and expressions. What if, for various reasons, we are simply missing the cues that Paul is arguing in a particular way? This, of course, is only a hypothesis. It cannot be proven that in 1 Corinthians 11 Paul is using a rhetorical device where he includes the argument of his opponents in order to refute it. The reason that it cannot be proven is that there is no signal given in the text by Paul that this is what he is doing. However, if this is an accepted method of argumentation, it is possible that there are simply clues in the text rather than overt statements of intent. Let us propose, for the sake of argument, that this might be the case, and follow the argument through.

It is not at all unlikely, as we are only party to "half a conversation," that we might be missing the cues. If we know that Paul cites the Corinthians elsewhere, and we know that this is an accepted form of argumentation, then let us propose that this might be the case and examine the text as a carefully crafted debate, in which Paul juxtaposes two irreconcilable positions, the Corinthian one arguing that women *should* wear head coverings (which the Corinthians would have been well aware of as it was their own argument), and his own position arguing against them, in order to demonstrate the flawed logic and absurdity of one in the face of the other, and to censure them for enforcing this as a practice. Let us turn to the passage itself.

39. Ibid., 540.

40. Ibid.

41. Ibid., 541.

The Teaching of Paul

Christ is the κεφαλὴ of Man

² ἐπαινῶ δὲ ὑμᾶς ὅτι πάντα μου μέμνησθε καὶ καθὼς παρέδωκα ὑμῖν τὰς παραδόσεις κατέχετε. ³ θέλω δὲ ὑμᾶς εἰδέναι ὅτι παντὸς ἀνδρὸς ἡ κεφαλὴ ὁ χριστός ἐστιν, κεφαλὴ δὲ γυναικὸς ὁ ἀνήρ, κεφαλὴ δὲ τοῦ χριστοῦ ὁ θεός.

Possible translations of these verses include:

> I commend you/praise you because you remember me in everything and maintain the traditions just as I handed them on to you/even as I delivered them to you. But I want you to understand/realize (or "But I would have you know") that the head of every man is Christ, the head of a woman/the woman is man/her husband, and the head of Christ is God.

Paul begins by praising the Corinthians for keeping to the traditions that he has handed on to them. As Paul quite clearly goes on to censure them, this verse has posed problems for interpreters. What precisely is he praising them for? Although this is sometimes understood to be an instance of irony or sarcasm, it is more likely that this is a genuine word of praise for the Corinthians. If we accept this as genuine, then verse 3 following would be an example of Pauline teaching that he did indeed pass on to them in the first place and that they also still adhere to in some form. The problem might be, however, that they have taken some of his teaching, but then gone on to modify that teaching to serve their own ends, hence the praise for keeping to his teaching, but the censure to follow. Whereas verse 3 is often read straightforwardly as Paul's view, stated in order to correct the Corinthians, I propose that there is much more subtlety in Paul's citing of this tripartite formula at the beginning of his argument. My proposal, therefore, is that Paul has indeed taught them that Christ is the κεφαλὴ of man and that man is the κεφαλὴ of woman, and that they themselves also teach this, but that Paul had intended this to be understood in a particular way that the Corinthians have lost sight of. Thus he reiterates his teaching, clarifying the language of "head" in the light of the truth that "God is the κεφαλὴ of Christ," which is to be the key pairing. There are four reasons that I would offer for reading verse 3 in this light. The first is textual: how the sentence is constructed. The second is based on early readings of this verse, which I believe quite rightly place exegetical limits on how we may read the language of "head" in relation to each couplet. The third stems from the God/Christ language in the rest of 1 Corinthians, and the fourth is a reference to chapter 12, where Paul explicates his teaching on the nature of the "body," which I suggest is directly relevant to his use of "head" in verse 3.

A Qualifying Clause

Paul uses a particular construction in verse 3 indicating a mild form of correction rather than a straightforward rebuke, or the introduction of something new. He begins, "I praise you for remembering the traditions/teaching as I passed them/it on to you." He carries on, "But I want you to understand . . . ." That Paul begins verse 3 with this phrase "I want you to understand . . ." rather than "Do you not know . . ." (οὐκ οἴδατε) is significant. The latter is a common phrase in 1 Corinthians preceding a Pauline corrective, occurring in 3:16; 5:6; 6:2, 3, 9, 15, 16, 19; 9:13, 24. An alternative introductory phrase for a corrective might also have been "I do not wish you to be ignorant . . ." (οὐ θέλω γὰρ ὑμᾶς ἀγνοεῖν 10:1; 12:1). Instead, Paul employs a different phrase, which is not a straightforward instruction or statement of dogma, or a rebuke, but a clarifying and qualifying statement. Furthermore, the verb form Paul uses for "know" or "understand" (εἰδέναι) is the perfect active infinitive, referring then to completed events with present consequences. Thus we might render the phrase more precisely, "I wish/want you to have understood/known . . " preceded by what Fee notes is an adversative "but."[1] It could also be that he follows this with

1. There are only two other instances of Paul using εἰδέναι in his letters. In 1 Cor

a quote, which could be signaled by the use of "that" (ὅτι), but we cannot prove this. Finally, that Paul chooses to use the tripartite formula in an unusual order should cause us to question why. The fact that he ends the phrase with God/Christ rather than beginning with this indicates the emphasis on the final couplet.

I am proposing that by beginning the section in this way, Paul is addressing a misunderstanding among the Corinthians of his own teaching on men and women that he had at one time passed on to them, and which they themselves adhere to, but in a corrupt form. In other words, Bristow's point regarding Paul's thought as interpreted through a subordinationist lens is apposite. We might understand Paul in verses 2–3 to be communicating something akin to the following: "I praise you for remembering the traditions that I passed on to you regarding Christ as the head of man and man as the head of woman. However, I want you to know that when I say that Christ is the head of every man, and man is the head of woman, you must also understand that God is the head of Christ." What might Paul be wishing to clarify by including this phrase?

The Meaning of κεφαλὴ

The meaning of κεφαλὴ has received extensive attention from scholars and it would be impossible to cover the arguments here. They are well documented in many commentaries. The possible translations include ruler, leader, person in authority, foremost, one who is preeminent, and source. It is very difficult for us to know precisely what Paul means when using the word here. What I wish to do in this section is to highlight the problems associated with certain exegetical options and note what he cannot mean, before offering some tentative suggestions as to what Paul might be communicating by the use of κεφαλὴ language here.

It is possible that Paul is adding his own qualifying and controlling couplet to the Corinthians' use of what was taught by him in the first place.

2:2 he uses this verb form in the same way as in 11:3, writing, οὐ γὰρ ἔκρινα τι εἰδέναι ἐν ὑμῖν εἰ μὴ Ἰησοῦν Χριστὸν καὶ τοῦτον ἐσταυρωμένον. "For I decided to know nothing [not to know anything] among you except Jesus Christ, and him crucified." Here then he is also referring to a past event with present consequences. In 1 Thess 5:12 it is used in a different way, ἐρωτῶμεν δὲ ὑμᾶς, ἀδελφοί, εἰδέναι τοὺς κοπιῶντας ἐν ὑμῖν καὶ προϊσταμένους ὑμῶν ἐν κυρίῳ καὶ νουθετοῦντας ὑμᾶς. "But we appeal to you, brothers and sisters, to respect those who labour among you, and have charge of you in the Lord and admonish you."

Regardless of whether this is the case or not, that God is the κεφαλὴ of Christ must be the hermeneutical key to the other pairings, and so we should start there. Despite insistence by some that κεφαλὴ most certainly means ruler, leader, or person in authority, if we wish to use it in this sense, there are two further questions that we then have to face. The first is whether this can be simply applied in a univocal sense to the nature of God. The second is how we may then apply what we claim to be true of the nature of the God/Christ relation to the Christ/man relation and also to the man/woman relation. This brings us to a potential dispute between the systematic theologian and the biblical scholar in our language about God.

Whereas a systematic theologian will often refer to patristic debates in order to seek an exegetical solution for biblical texts regarding the nature of God, it is commonly claimed among biblical scholars that bringing creedal categories to bear on scriptural statements is anachronistic and/or inadmissible. We should accept the text on its own terms. Lakey, for example, insists that to bring Nicene categories to bear upon the exegesis of 1 Corinthians 11:3 is "hermeneutically naïve and exegetically unsatisfactory."[2] However, Payne notes that those who fail to refer to Nicene categories inevitably end up with a subordinationist Christology, emphatically rejected in very early readings of this verse on the grounds that it was Arian. "Chrysostom, Theodoret, and Theophylact emphasize the misuses of 1 Cor 11:3 by Arians and others to subordinate the present, eternal, or ontological Christ to the Father." Chrysostom's reading of this verse rules out certain conclusions both with respect to the nature of God and to the relation of the nature of human relations to God and to one another.

> "But the head of the woman is the man; and the head of Christ is God." Here the heretics rush upon us with a certain declaration of inferiority, which out of these words they contrive against the Son. But they stumble against themselves. For if "the man be the head of the woman," and the head be of the same substance with the body, and "the head of Christ is God," the Son is of the same substance with the Father. "Nay," say they, "it is not His being of another substance which we intend to show from hence, but that He is under subjection." What then are we to say to this? In the first place, when any thing lowly is said of him conjoined as He is with the Flesh, there is no disparagement of the Godhead in what is said, the Economy admitting the expression. However, tell me how thou intendest to prove this from the passage? "Why, as the

2. Lakey, *Image and Glory*, 180.

man governs the wife," saith he, "so also the Father, Christ." Therefore also as Christ governs the man, so likewise the Father, the
Son. "For the head of every man," we read, "is Christ." And who
could ever admit this? For if the superiority of the Son compared
with us, be the measure of the Father's compared with the Son,
consider to what meanness thou wilt bring Him.[3]

Chrysostom makes two main points: the first regarding what is permissible to claim vis-à-vis the nature of the Godhead in Christ; the second
what it is permissible to claim vis-à-vis the analogy between the God/Christ
relation and the man/woman/wife relation. Thus, Chrysostom first argues
that we cannot claim that the Son is inferior to the Father in any sense as
"the Son is of the same substance with the Father." If comments such as
these are deemed anachronistic, this will leave the systematic theologian
and the biblical scholar at an impasse, especially if the point is pressed too
hard, as Lakey appears to do. The creedal confession that the Father is God,
the Son is God, and the Spirit is God is surely admissible as a hermeneutical
tool in this instance as long as it can be shown to be consistent with Paul's
theology expressed elsewhere. While such a demonstration lies beyond the
scope of this work, the mere allegation of anachronism is not sufficient by
itself to dissuade us from accepting Chrysostom's point. Chrysostom is not
alone in the tradition in supposing that Trinitarian ways of thinking shed
genuine light on the meaning of biblical texts. Having ruled out concepts
such as superiority/inferiority and ruling over/ruled in the Godhead, we
cannot, however, eliminate the concept of submission and even subjection,
as these themes emerge in 1 Corinthians 15 in the God/Christ language
and relation. The incarnate Son is given authority to subdue and destroy
the rulers, authorities, and powers, and then comes under the one who has
subjected all things, God. Despite obvious hierarchical concepts functioning here, it is essential not to lose sight of the truth that the Son too is God.
This is what the Fathers of the church consistently attempt to convey. We
will return to this.

What of the implications of this for Christ/man and man/woman?
Chrysostom goes on to his second point, highlighting our second problem,
which is to demonstrate the flaws in drawing a straightforward analogy
between the nature of the relationship between Christ as the "head" of man
and God as the "head" of Christ, and to issue a salutary warning against

---

3. Chrysostom, *Hom.*, 26.3.

inferring a direct equivalence of the God/Christ relation to the Christ/man or the man/woman relation from this one verse.

> So that we must not try all things by like measure in respect of ourselves and of God, though the language used concerning them be similar; but we must assign to God a certain appropriate excellency, and so great as belongs to God. For should they not grant this, many absurdities will follow. As thus; "the head of Christ is God:" and, "Christ is the head of the man, and he of the woman." Therefore if we choose to take the term "head" in the like sense in all the clauses, the Son will be as far removed from the Father as we are from Him. Nay, and the woman will be as far removed from us as we are from the Word of God. And what the Son is to the Father, this both we are to the Son and the woman again to the man. And who will endure this?[4]

Chrysostom cautions against applying "head" in a univocal sense to all three relations, lest we stumble into the inevitable errant conclusions that arise in respect of the relation of the Son to the Father, the Son to man, and man to woman. We should be careful of the many absurdities that might follow. Finally, he rules out one further cause of erroneous, subordinationist readings by pointing out that if Paul meant to speak of subjection, the relation between man and woman or "husband" and "wife" does not constitute a very convincing example.

> But dost thou understand the term "head" differently in the case of the man and the woman, from what thou dost in the case of Christ? Therefore in the case of the Father and the Son, must we understand it differently also. "How understand it differently?" saith the objector. According to the occasion. For had Paul meant to speak of rule and subjection, as thou sayest, he would not have brought forward the instance of a wife, but rather of a slave and a master. For what if the wife be under subjection to us? It is as a wife, as free, as equal in honor. And the Son also, though He did become obedient to the Father, it was as the Son of God, it was as God. For as the obedience of the Son to the Father is greater than we find in men towards the authors of their being, so also His liberty is greater.[5]

He goes on to note that woman is subjected to man not at creation, where they are bone of bone and flesh of flesh, but at the fall, when woman

4. Ibid.
5. Ibid.

"made ill use of her privilege," became an "ensnarer" and "ruined all!" She clearly got what she deserved then in having to be subject to her husband from then on. Note that for Chrysostom, the subordination of woman to man is part of the fall, *not part of creation*. Despite the unfortunate moment of blaming the demise of the human race on the woman, Chrysostom goes on wisely to warn against a literal or particular reading of this verse and to accept "the notion of a perfect union and the first principle" with respect to the God/Christ relation. So Chrysostom reads the language of κεφαλὴ *in relation to* God and Christ as denoting a perfect union of the Father and the Son and the Father as the first principle or *arche*, which is never intended to denote hierarchy, or even precedence in the eternal Godhead. However, he warns against extrapolating these ideas "absolutely" and applying them directly to a man-woman relationship because when applied to the God-head the notions are too high for us to grasp, "the union is surer and the beginning more honorable." Precisely. We may not simply read off from the language of "head" when applied to God/Christ and apply it first to Christ/ man and then to man/woman, even though we may draw out some simi- larities. Murphy-O'Connor cites Cyril of Alexandria in a similar vein. Cyril brings out both similarity and difference in the use of κεφαλὴ in all three instances. "Thus we say that the *kephale* of every man is Christ, because he was excellently made through him. And the *kephale* of woman is man, because she was taken from his flesh. Likewise, the *kephale* of Christ is God, because He is from Him according to nature."[6] According to Cyril, κεφαλὴ is used in three similar but different ways, all denoting origin and relation.

Whatever κεφαλὴ does mean, it does *not* mean that as God rules over Christ, Christ rules over man, and man rules over woman, because we can- not claim that God rules over Christ in the first place. It may be that with Cyril, we can make a claim for κεφαλὴ being used in this context to denote origin and relation, as long as we acknowledge that the origins and rela- tion that we are speaking of are of a different order when applied to God/ Christ, Christ/man, and man/woman. The Son is eternally begotten; the man and woman are created. There is a time when they were not. Man is not "of one substance" with Christ as the Son is of the Father; neither is man the creator of woman as Christ is of man. We should also note here the problems associated with the translation of "man" that we encounter in verse 7. Which man is Paul referring to: all men, or only those who are

6. Cyril of Alexandria, (*Ad. Arcadiam* 1.1.5.5(2).63), cited in Murphy-O'Connor, *Keys*, 191.

"in Christ"? Possibly we could imagine Paul to be speaking of some kind of first principle and perfect union with respect to God/Christ and some kind of first principle with respect to Christ/man and man/woman according to Genesis 2. We should be cautious here though, bearing in mind that this can only be explained in the light of Genesis 2 and not from Genesis 1, and that we are very unsure about what Paul is saying regarding the relationship of Christ to man.

Whatever we decide upon with respect to the meaning of κεφαλὴ, we should bear in mind the fact that Paul deliberately chooses what Thiselton calls a "polymorphous concept" with multiple meanings from context to context, an observation that is certainly borne out even in this short but remarkably complex verse. We should also remember that, in keeping with the rest of Paul's theology, and particularly the theology expressed in 1 and 2 Corinthians, neither man nor woman, whatever their position, would be able to distance themselves from a full identification with the crucified Christ. If Paul's original teaching on Christ and man and woman had been extrapolated by the Corinthian Christians along the lines of a theology of glory (for the man and imputed glory for the woman), shame (for the woman) and honor, superiority and inferiority, and applied in literal terms with respect to the heads of men and women manifested in the wearing (or not) of head coverings, then we may be seeing here Paul's attempt to correct that misconception, which he comes to from verse 11 onwards. Paul develops his own teaching on men and women in terms of provenance and relationship, not in terms of a hierarchical ontology, but in terms of mutuality and interdependence, as we will go on to see. Admittedly here, whatever we make of the κεφαλὴ language, it appears that woman is the κεφαλὴ of no one, but Paul will come to this point in due course and correct any mistaken view that the creation narrative in Genesis 2 either negates the generative role of woman or, crucially, the dependence of man upon her for his existence. In order to explore further what Paul may have been communicating with the κεφαλὴ language in verse 3 we will examine other instances of God/Christ language in 1 Corinthians as well as references to the "body" in chapter 12.

So that God may be all in all

Paul's use of God/Christ language in 1 Corinthians is often noted, as is his emphasis on the all-encompassing nature of God. Thiselton cites J. Moffatt when commenting on 15:28, who himself believed that Paul in this verse is attacking a "form of Christ-mysticism which loosened the nexus between God and Christ."[7] Thiselton writes that Moffatt

> explains the so-called subordinationism of the God-Christ relationship in this epistle in different terms. He proposes that, surrounded by cozy cult deities of the mystery cults and Graeco-Roman religion, the church at Corinth too readily appropriated a "Lord Jesus" cult mind-set without sufficiently "serious reverence for a supreme deity over the universe," viewing "God" as a shadowing figure in contrast to the passionate, intimate, devotion offered by others to Serapis or Asclepios or by Christians to Jesus as Lord.[8]

Fee also refers to Moffatt as identifying a Graeco-Roman tendency to gather around a heroic or divine figure without the inclusion of any serious reverence "for a supreme, central deity."[9] Paul's emphasis on "God" in this case would be specifically to correct this imbalance. Whether this was the case or not is not verifiable; however, the emphasis that Paul places on the supremacy of God, and on the all-encompassing nature of God, even in relation to Christ, in this epistle is undeniable.

Thiselton notes in 1:2 that τοῦ θεοῦ is possessive, serving Paul's point that the church belongs solely to God, and therefore, not to any factions or domineering leaders. He writes, "[t]he church, Paul insists, belongs not to the wealthy, or to 'patrons,' or to some self-styled inner circle of 'spiritual people who manifest gifts,' *but to God*."[10] This is a crucial point, and one which we will return to with respect to Paul's picture of the body in chapter 12. Thiselton goes on, "[t]he church is *God's* growing 'field,' *God's* planned 'construction,' *God's* inner shrine (1 Cor. 3:9) where θεοῦ, **of God**, stands three times in an emphatic word order."[11] "Karl Barth captures the tone magnificently: 'The main defect' at Corinth was the belief of the addressees 'not in God, but in their own belief in God and in particular leaders.'"[12] Citing Jüngel, Thiselton writes,

---

7. Moffatt, *First Epistle*, 250–51, cited in Thiselton, *The First Epistle*, 68.

8. Moffatt, *First Epistle*, 250, cited in Thiselton, *The First Epistle*, 804.

9. Fee, *First Epistle*, 1237.

10. Thiselton, *The First Epistle*, 73.

11. Ibid., 74.

12. Barth, *The Resurrection of the Dead*, 17, cited in Thiselton, *The First Epistle*, 74.

On the one side, the cross is "the power of **God**" (1 Cor 1:18); things are what they are "through the will of God" (1:1), through the decree, choice, or election of God (1:21, 27, 28; 2:7, 9); life and growth depend on the agency of God (3:6,7); everything awaits the verdict of God (4:5); the assignment of varied "gifts" and even "modes of existence" (or "bodies") depends on God's decision (12:28; 15:10, 38). On the other side, Paul sees God's self-disclosure in the crucified Jesus.[13]

At the same time, God was in Christ, reconciling the world to himself (2 Cor 5:19). All things come from God, including the salvation of the Corinthians (1:30; 8:6; 11:30). All things are destined for God (8:6; 15:28), Christ himself comes from God (1:30; 11:3), owes allegiance to God (3:23; 11:3; 15:28), and Paul refers also to the Spirit as the Spirit of God, not the Spirit of Christ (2:10–14; 3:16; 6:11; 7:40; 12:3). If I am correct in positing that the God/Christ couplet is inserted by Paul as the final couplet in the tripartite κεφαλὴ formula in order to address a christological and anthropological heresy that had arisen in the Corinthian church, then this emphasis on God would support that theory. In 3:23, Paul writes, ὑμεῖς δὲ Χριστοῦ, Χριστὸς δὲ θεοῦ, "You are of Christ, and Christ is of God." In 4:1 he writes, "So let us reckon ourselves as servants of Christ and stewards of the mystery of God." Whatever we decide with respect to κεφαλὴ in verse 3 we should take two Pauline views on God/Christ/man/woman into account. The first is in relation to creation and expressed in his summative statement in 11:12. Woman is made from man, man is born of woman, "And *all* things are from God." The second is eschatological: that all will be subsumed under the being of God, including man, woman, and Christ.

You are the "body" of Christ

That Paul is addressing the vexing reality of division within the Corinthian church is stated from the outset of the letter. I am suggesting that Paul's reference to the "head" in verse 3 is a reference to his teaching which has been corrupted by the Corinthians, perhaps especially in a way that has allowed a group of spiritually gifted men to overidentify with the glorious Christ, leading them to become domineering and divisive, and to implement practices aimed at controlling and/or silencing the women. In 11:3

13. Jüngel, *God as the Mystery of the World*, 156–57, cited in Thiselton, *The First Epistle*, 84.

Paul introduces the language of "head" as they would have been accustomed to hearing it and using it, but adding a qualifying clause. In chapter 12, he develops the language of the "body," and specifically the body of Christ, in order to describe the Corinthians' situation and to paint a certain picture for them as to how they should behave with one another. Chapter 12 is particularly illuminating with respect to Paul's thinking on the nature of the Christian church and how it should operate, but is also significant within the letter itself as it develops the theme of the language of the body. Through the metaphor of the physical body, Paul exhorts the congregation to elevate respect, love, interdependence, and care for one another over charismatic gifts or "roles." Not only this, but the overriding message of chapter 12 is that those who see themselves as more important and more worthy of honor should instead be honoring the inferior, the lowest, and the least. We have already noted this theme in chapters 2 and 4. Paul's teaching here is not simply that they should be honoring those who are perceived to be inferior, but that there is a God-ordained reversal of status in the body of Christ. "But *God has so adjusted the body*, giving the greater honor to the inferior part." What is the purpose of God having done this? It is "that there may be no discord in the body, but that the members may have the same care for one another. If one member suffers, all suffer together; if one member is honored/glorified, all rejoice together" (vv. 24–26). I suggest that Paul sets the context for the language of "head" within his picture of the "body" as well as in his theology of God/Christ. First, he warns those who perceive themselves to be in the position of the "head" that they may never say to any other part of the body, "I have no need of you." But second, and far more radically, Paul claims that those who are more "important" must devote themselves to honoring the dishonorable parts in the knowledge that those members are the ones accorded the highest honor by God himself.

In concluding this section on the language of κεφαλὴ, we should be aware of what we may and may not claim as possible meanings. First, we should be cautious of applying κεφαλὴ in a univocal sense to God/Christ, Christ/man, and man/woman, ensuring that we are aware of what we are claiming for each relation in each instance, and then in an analogous sense with respect to each couplet, one with another. Second, we should take into account Paul's God/Christ theology in the rest of his letter, in which he emphasizes the all-encompassing nature of God as the one in whom all creatures have their existence, and to whom all will return. Third, as Paul has introduced the language of "head" in 11:3 we should explore what he teaches on the "body" in chapter 12 with particular reference to the body of Christ. Here we see not simply an egalitarian picture of the members of the body of Christ, but one in which the least and the lowest enjoy the most honored position. It is an inversion of hierarchy. As we have previously discussed, the allusion here to the women, the slaves, the ones who are least gifted, and those on the bottom rung should most certainly not be lost.

Summary of κεφαλή

In summary, we are faced with a number of problems related to verse 3. The first is simply that we do not know precisely what Paul meant by this word, and therefore what he was trying to communicate by using it in relation to the Godhead, Christ, man, and woman. The second is that all attempts to apply one concept in all three pairings become highly problematic. The fact that Paul's teaching here is impenetrable to some extent could also give us some clues as to how it may have been misconstrued, even at the time. We are left, then, to piece our evidence together. I suggest that what Paul is doing in this chapter, and indeed, through the whole of the letter, is reframing his original teaching, partly for the sake of clarity, but more importantly because it had been used for the glorification of men and the oppression and exclusion of women. It is difficult to evade any hierarchical and/or sequential overtones to the language of *kephale* altogether—mostly because it is also difficult to divorce this language from the language of subjection of Christ to God that emerges in 1 Corinthians 15. Is Paul simply saying woman submits to man, man to Christ, Christ to God? It certainly could be read in that way, and indeed it often is, and therein lies the problem. Once we believe that Paul is committed to a hierarchical sequence of submission, it is hard to think he might have meant something else. I believe this was precisely the issue at Corinth that Paul is attempting to address here. So whereas his teaching could be open to the interpretation that woman is the last in the chain of submission, it is my opinion that in this letter he is framing the language of *kephale* to *prevent the concept from being understood in this way*. If it is used in this way, it becomes clear that it can then be used to undermine a woman's full participation in public worship and to convince her that she should be under her husband's or a man's authority. At the same time he targets man's predilection to take the language of *kephale* as some warrant for a self-inflated view of his own status and glory, all of which are elements of the fall. My reasons for this theory are fourfold.

The first is that he emphasizes the role of woman as progenitor of man in verse 12, demonstrating man's dependence on woman for his very existence. The woman too is equally dependent on man, thus neither gender can "lord" it over the other. The second is that he claims that woman has her own crowning glory intrinsic to her physical being (also interestingly on her head), *her hair*. Man is *not* her glory. The third is that in chapter 14, Paul will rebuke the Corinthian men for subjecting the wives to a passive role in church, and forcing them to learn through their husbands, with no voice of their own. The fourth is that submission is not a gendered concept, but a reality for men and women who choose to follow Christ. In other words, it seems that submission and even subjection are key concepts for Paul. He describes himself as a slave! However, I do not believe that he applies this to the man/woman or husband/wife relationship in any concrete form, either in the church or in the marriage. In fact, we have examples that speak of the opposite. From 1 Corinthians 7:1–15 we know that marriage is a relationship of mutuality and reciprocal authority. What is true for the husband is equally true for the wife. It seems though that in Paul's view, the Christian posture for both men and women should be one of submission and to take the lower part. This, I believe, is borne out throughout the letter. Once we understand this, we have understood a fundamental principle of the cruciform life. Man and woman are interdependent creatures, submitted to Christ, who though himself God, through his own subjection and obedience as the incarnate Son, will return all things, including us, to our ultimate "head." The "sequence" articulated in Paul's original teaching is now interpreted through his christological lens of the crucified Christ.

Every Man . . .

4 πᾶς ἀνὴρ προσευχόμενος ἢ προφητεύων κατὰ κεφαλῆς ἔχων καταισχύνει τὴν κεφαλὴν αὐτοῦ· 5 πᾶσα δὲ γυνὴ προσευχομένη ἢ προφητεύουσα ἀκατακαλύπτῳ τῇ κεφαλῇ καταισχύνει τὴν κεφαλὴν αὐτῆς· ἓν γάρ ἐστιν καὶ τὸ αὐτὸ τῇ ἐξυρημένῃ.

I have covered verse 4 in considerable detail above in terms of possible interpretations. I am suggesting here that this is the point where Paul does "quote" a Corinthian slogan. This is the Corinthian description and theological rationale for the practice that entails that women should have their heads covered in worship, and that men should have their heads uncovered. "Every man who prays or prophesies with his head covered dishonors his head. But every woman who prays or prophesies with her head uncovered dishonors her head—it is the same as having her head shaved" (NIV). It is possible that the Corinthians are referring here both to hair length and head coverings. Chrysostom assumes that Paul is speaking of long hair on men as well as a head covering, and head coverings for women, in preparation for what will come later in verse 14.[14] This would make more sense of this verse, and solve the intractable problem of deciding between the two. If the Corinthians believed that long hair on a man was dishonoring to Christ, and that a bare head was shameful on a woman, this would resolve some of the problems with the passage. It also makes more sense of the text if we ascribe the Corinthian view to a flawed theology of creation, including an overlay of a Stoic view of "the nature of things," but I will come back to that point below.

In order to reconstruct the Corinthian argument, we only need to draw on many of the traditional readings that we have surveyed, and then simply transpose them from Paul's point of view to that of the Corinthians. It appears that they are claiming that men—as the glory of God, with Christ as their metaphorical "head," and as the metaphorical "head" of woman—must pray with their literal heads uncovered (or with short hair) in order to not dishonor Christ. Women, conversely, and in their subordinate role, must pray with their literal heads covered, in order not to dishonor their metaphorical "head," man. This is supported by verses 7–10. Of course, as with every other interpretation, we are now in the realm of speculation because we do not have access to their thinking, but we do know that a literal interpretation of what should or should not be on a head was derived from a metaphorical concept of spiritual glory and authority[15]—this is true whoever we believe to be putting forward the argument.

A Total Disgrace

[6] εἰ γὰρ οὐ κατακαλύπτεται γυνή, καὶ κειράσθω· εἰ δὲ αἰσχρὸν γυναικὶ τὸ κείρασθαι ἢ ξυρᾶσθαι, κατακαλυπτέσθω.

14. Chrysostom, *Hom.*, 26.2.
15. See Fee, *First Epistle*, 499.

In my reading, I posit that verse 6 is in fact the voice of Paul mimicking the Corinthian threat in order to expose the underlying absurdity, and possibly even the aggression of their argument. "For if a woman will not veil herself, then she should cut off her hair; but if it is disgraceful for a woman to have her hair cut off or to be shaved, she should wear a veil." If a woman prays with her head uncovered, she is dishonoring her head (God, men, the angels?), which presumably the Corinthians were arguing is as bad as a woman appearing in public with a shaved head—a sign of severe disgrace. Had they perhaps even threatened to cut someone's hair off? But if she cuts her hair off or shaves her head, she will be disgraced, so the solution—she should cover her head. He is taking their argument to its logical, shocking conclusion. If you force women to wear head coverings, and they refuse to comply, you might as well shave their heads. If this is the Corinthians' argument, Paul exposes the abusive nature of it, and the coercion behind it. If you refuse to cover your head, you are behaving like a prostitute, so you should have your head shaved. But if you do have your head shaved, then you will be known to be a prostitute, so you should cover your head. Chrysostom regards this verse as a rhetorical *reductio ad absurdum*: "If you cast away the 'covering' appointed by divine law, then cast away the 'covering' appointed by nature. . . . Thereby she falls from her proper honor."[16] I too would argue that this is an example of a *reductio ad absurdum*, although I understand it to be applied by Paul to the Corinthian argument in order to expose the flaws in the Corinthian view.

The Corinthian Man's Glory

7 ἀνὴρ μὲν γὰρ οὐκ ὀφείλει κατακαλύπτεσθαι τὴν κεφαλήν, εἰκὼν καὶ δόξα θεοῦ ὑπάρχων· ἡ γυνὴ δὲ δόξα ἀνδρός ἐστιν. 8 οὐ γάρ ἐστιν ἀνὴρ ἐκ γυναικός, ἀλλὰ γυνὴ ἐξ ἀνδρός· 9 καὶ γὰρ οὐκ ἐκτίσθη ἀνὴρ διὰ τὴν γυναῖκα, ἀλλὰ γυνὴ διὰ τὸν ἄνδρα. 10 διὰ τοῦτο ὀφείλει ἡ γυνὴ ἐξουσίαν ἔχειν ἐπὶ τῆς κεφαλῆς διὰ τοὺς ἀγγέλους.

7 For a man ought not to have his head veiled, since he is the image and reflection of God; but woman is the reflection of man. 8 Indeed, man was not made from woman, but woman from man. 9 Neither was man created for the sake of woman, but woman for the sake of

---

16. Chrysostom, *Hom.*, 26.4.

man. **10** For this reason a woman ought to have a symbol of authority on her head, because of the angels.

7 A man ought not to cover his head, since he is the image and glory of God; but woman is the glory of man. **8** For man did not come from woman, but woman from man; **9** neither was man created for woman, but woman for man. **10** It is for this reason that a woman ought to have authority over her own head, because of the angels. (NIV)

If this is now understood as the voice of the Corinthians, it becomes much clearer why there is a corrupted form of Genesis 1:26–27. The Corinthian prophetic leaders and teachers who claim that they "have the word of God" are teaching that men are the image and glory of God, and that women are merely the image and glory of man—the perfect rationale for the subordination of women and the superiority of men. This theology of glory has superseded any sense of what it means for both men and women to be in Christ. This, and a particular understanding of an angelic presence in worship, underpins their view that the wearing of head coverings for women was honoring for God, men, and the angels. Moreover, this would also serve as the perfect rationale, not just for head coverings, but for keeping women silent before their husbands, as they must necessarily adopt a subordinate role, but we will come to that in due course. Interestingly Payne commenting on this passage toys with the idea that it might represent a Corinthian slogan, but ultimately dismisses it. These are his reasons:

> If ὑπάρχων ("since he is") in 11:7 gives a reason "to cover," "man as male is the image and glory of God" would express a Corinthian slogan used to defend display of effeminate hair. This slogan fits perfectly with the exaltation of the male body that typifies homosexual display, the Corinthians' view of their own exalted status, their pride in their sexual freedom, their haughty spirit, and their overly realized eschatology. If Paul here quotes a Corinthian slogan, this explains why "man as male" (ἀνήρ) is used rather than the inclusive term "humankind" (ἄνθρωπος), as in Paul's other affirmations of the "image of God in man," why man is the image of God (elsewhere man is made in the image of God, whereas Christ alone is the image of God, 2 Cor 4:4; Col 1:15), and why man *is* the glory of God (difficult to reconcile with Rom 1:23; 3:23; 5:2).[17]

17. Payne, *Man and Woman*, 176.

Payne quite correctly identifies a number of problems in this phrase "man" as the image and glory of God. In the end, however, he rejects these musings and opts for the idea that this glory theology accords with Paul's high Christology.[18]

If we do believe this phrase to be Pauline, we have to accept that Paul is expressing here a theology of derivation—that woman is derivative of man. For one thing to be derived from another places the derived object in a dependent or descendant position. It is true that in the story of Eve being brought out of Adam's side, that the woman is "derived" from man. However, with reference to this narrative, if woman is derivative of man then man is derivative of the dust, not of Christ. Thus, even with reference to this narrative, the theology is problematic. This is further complicated by the narratives in Genesis, which we have already referred to, that portray the simultaneous creation of man and woman by God and the creation of man by woman with the help of God. These narratives conform most happily with Paul's claims in verse 11–16, rendering the claims in verses 8–9 not only anomalous but out of line with the story of the creation of man and woman in the Christian tradition. I suggest therefore, that this has nothing to do with Paul's high Christology or a misplaced theology of derivation, but that it is a Corinthian christological and anthropological heresy, that Paul is totally and adamantly in disagreement with them, and that in verse 11 he turns to his own argument in order to refute theirs.

Man and Woman

11 πλὴν οὔτε γυνὴ χωρὶς ἀνδρὸς οὔτε ἀνὴρ χωρὶς γυναικὸς ἐν κυρίῳ· **12** ὥσπερ γὰρ ἡ γυνὴ ἐκ τοῦ ἀνδρός, οὕτως καὶ ὁ ἀνὴρ διὰ τῆς γυναικός· τὰ δὲ πάντα ἐκ τοῦ θεοῦ.

11 Nevertheless, in the Lord woman is not independent of man or man independent of woman. **12** For just as woman came from man, so man comes through woman; but all things come from God.

11 Nevertheless, in the Lord woman is not independent of man, nor is man independent of woman. For as woman came from man, so also man is born of woman. **12** For as woman came from man, so also man is born of woman. But everything comes from God. (NIV)

18. Ibid., 178.

The third main clue then occurs in verse 11. Shoemaker writes,

> Another term that should be noted is *plen* v. 11. Although gener-
> ally translated "only" or "nevertheless," I believe this particle takes
> on a special rhetorical function for Paul. Although used only four
> times in his letters (Philippians 1:18; 3:16; 4:14; and here), it ap-
> pears to serve as a pointer in each case to an important statement.
> It is a term that introduces Paul's central theme in each context.
> Thus, I have chosen to render it "The point is."[19]

The point that Paul is making most emphatically, therefore, is the following: that "in the Lord woman is not independent of man, nor is man indepen-
dent of woman. For as woman came from man, so also man is born of woman." Paul overturns their patriarchal reading of creation. There is no hierarchy, neither is woman dependent on man, but both man and woman are interdependent, they are not "apart" from one another. That Paul is making a decisive break in the flow of thought and argument here is well supported.

There are a number of pointers that separate verses 2–10 from verses 11–16. We have already noted Payne's critique of verse 9. Lakey points out that verse 9 is not a biblical quote but that in verse 12a the form of expres-
sion corresponds to that of the LXX.[20] He says that "[t]he second of Paul's warrants (v. 9), not itself a biblical allusion, is an inference on the basis of the narrative sequence of the second creation story. Since woman was taken from (ἐκ) man because his solitude was not good (Gen. 2:18), she is for him and, for Paul, this means that she is to be his δόξα." Paul goes on to give a very, very different picture in verses 11–16. "In the Lord," the creation hierarchy is replaced by reciprocity. The question as we noted it above is what do we do with these contradictory pictures? Lakey rejects any supersession in the second half, commenting that "[t]his is not a reversal of the argument, but a careful qualification."[21] Lakey puts great weight on the prepositions both in Galatians 4:4 and in 1 Corinthians 11. As Paul has described Christ as γενόμεν ἐκ γυναικός (born of a woman) in Galatians 4:4 but here only uses the preposition διὰ (through a woman), Lakey believes this to signal that Paul means to denote the woman's inferiority. Woman is the instrumental cause of man and man is the material and final cause of

19. Shoemaker, "Unveiling," 61–62.
20. Lakey, *Image and Glory*, 114.
21. Ibid., 116.

woman. In this view, the complementarity in 1 Corinthians is still strictly hierarchical.

In my opinion, Lakey is stretching the point here. Paul's teaching in this section appears to be clear. Lest men believe that it is through them only that the image is borne and through them only that the image is transmitted, Paul makes it very clear that it is through woman that man is created and ἐκ (out of) woman that Christ is born. Payne makes the point that χωρὶς should be translated different, distinct, separated, set apart from. In all but four of Paul's sixteen uses, it is used to mean this (Rom 3:21, 28; 4:6; 7:8–9; 10:14; 1 Cor 4:8; 2 Cor 11:28; 12:3; Eph 2:12). Payne writes, "Paul is the first writer known to derive theological significance from the fact that every man is born through woman."[22] Moreover, God is not over man so that man can then be over woman, but God is over all, "But everything comes from (ἐκ) God" (ὥσπερ γὰρ ἡ γυνὴ ἐκ τοῦ ἀνδρὸς, οὕτως καὶ ὁ ἀνὴρ διὰ τῆς γυναικός· τὰ δὲ πάντα ἐκ τοῦ θεοῦ). Thiselton translates verses 11–12 "For just as woman had her origin from man even so man derives his existence through woman; and the source of everything is God." And as we noted above, Genesis 4:1 supports this view. Crucially, and as Paul explains in the rest of the letter, equality and interdependence function not only in creation, but also in Christ, because of the baptism of the Spirit. This view is also supported by Paul's portrait of marriage in 1 Corinthians 7 where, in a radically countercultural move, Paul declares that "a wife has authority over her husband's body" (1 Cor 7:4). It is extremely hard to refute the idea that the picture of man and woman "in the Lord" is radically different from the picture of woman as man's glory.

"Judge for yourselves"

13 Ἐν ὑμῖν αὐτοῖς κρίνατε· πρέπον ἐστὶν γυναῖκα ἀκατακάλυπτον τῷ θεῷ προσεύχεσθαι;

In the light of this, Paul throws the argument back on to them. "Judge for yourselves: is it proper for a woman to pray to God with her head uncovered/unveiled?" Thiselton notes the aorist in the Greek verb κρίνω is used to mean "to *reach a decision* and not to go on vacillating."[23] Paul has lost his patience with them on this issue. Lakey is in agreement with Thisel-

---

22. Payne, *Man and Woman*, 195.
23. Thiselton, *First Corinthians*, 176.

ton, although unwittingly makes a point about the language that serves my perspective that Paul is addressing the domineering men.

> The use of the aorist imperative κρίνατε signals not an open-ended process of deliberation, but rather a moment of decision; it is now time for the Corinthians to make up their minds. . . . The masculine plural pronoun αὐτοῖς, rather than αὐταῖς, signals that this is not a decision left to the uncovered Corinthian women; their attire is a matter for the entire congregation, or perhaps its leaders.[24]

Two further linguistic anomalies here are that in verse 13 Paul now only refers to praying and not to praying and prophesying and here avoids the language of shame and honor by using the word πρέπον (fitting) instead. The question he is asking the Corinthian men is simply this: "Is it fitting for a woman to pray to God with her head uncovered?" By this point he is expecting the answer, "Of course it is." He will then go on to reinforce his point using their own arguments against them.

The Nature of Things

[14] οὐδὲ ἡ φύσις αὐτὴ διδάσκει ὑμᾶς ὅτι ἀνὴρ μὲν ἐὰν κομᾷ ἀτιμία αὐτῷ ἐστιν, [15] γυνὴ δὲ ἐὰν κομᾷ δόξα αὐτῇ ἐστιν; ὅτι ἡ κόμη ἀντὶ περιβολαίου δέδοται αὐτῇ.

[14] Does not nature itself teach you that if a man wears long hair, it is degrading to him, [15] but if a woman has long hair it is her glory? For her hair is given to her for a covering.

[14] Does not the very nature of things teach you that if a man has long hair it is a disgrace to him, [15] but that if a woman has long hair it is her glory? For long hair is given to her instead of a covering. (NIV)

Paul's use of φύσις (nature) here is unusual. Thiselton notes four possible interpretations of this.

1. an intuitive or inborn sense of what is fitting, right, or seemly
2. the way humans are created
3. the physical reality of how the creation is ordered

---

24. Lakey, *Image and Glory*, 117.

4. the customs of a given society[25]

He makes the point that Paul would have been aware of contemporary resonances in the Graeco-Roman world to the ordering of how things are, but that the Hebrew usage of nature would be more like "God's ordering of the world by his command."[26]

There is no real consensus on what Paul might have meant by "the nature of things." It is possible though that he is referring to a Stoic use of the term. Lakey writes: "Moreover, this passage also contains the only instance of the Greek term φύσις (1 Cor. 11:14) in the entire epistle. This again is significant because, as has been noted, the Stoicizing influences to which the Corinthian 'strong' appear to be liable *make it likely that this word would have been part of their repertoire of material and cosmological terminology.*"[27] He goes on to add that Paul's response to the issue of gendered attire "falls squarely into Stoic discourses concerning natural sexual differences." This confuses him however. "This of course begs the question of why Paul enjoins integration into the gendered structures of the cosmos when he elsewhere rejects assimilation outright; does he speak out of both sides of the mouth?"[28] Murphy-O'Connor also notes that the Stoics dignified social conventions as the teaching of "nature."[29] Why is Paul using the Stoic discourse?

Could it be that Paul is addressing the Corinthians using their own language and thought? Paige writes:

> The question I wish to raise is *not* whether or not *Paul* thought in Stoic manner; rather, could it be that he is writing to people who themselves use such language, think in a Stoicizing manner, or are impressed with Stoic ideas? Otherwise why does he so frequently use language that appears Stoic, though he operates with different assumptions? After all, the manner of Paul's expression is not shaped solely by his Jewish background and Christian confession, but surely to some extent by the needs of his audience as well? Do not their problems, vocabulary, and level of understanding influence the manner of the apostle's communication with them?[30]

25. Thiselton, *The First Epistle*, 844.

26. Ibid., 845.

27. Lakey, *Image and Glory*, 96 (my italics).

28. Ibid.

29. Murphy-O'Connor, *Keys*, 150.

30. Paige, "Stoicism," 209.

As a final proposal, which is purely a tentative suggestion, but one that I think the previous observations support, I propose that Paul is referring to one of their own ideas about hairstyles and nature, but using the idea slightly tongue in cheek as a final coup de grace.

This reading of verse 14 as somewhat ironic is supported by the allusion to Paul cutting his hair or shaving his head upon leaving Corinth as a result of a vow that he had taken while he was there (Acts 18:18). This enigmatic statement has left commentators puzzled as to the nature of the vow that Paul took, but as it entailed leaving his hair to grow, the most obvious solution is that Paul took a Nazirite vow while he was in Corinth. If this were the case, then Paul would have been growing his hair for eighteen months, meaning *he would have had long hair while in Corinth!* He certainly would not have had short hair. He only cut it, or shaved it off, when he left them. Even if this is not a reference to a Nazirite vow, which it may not be, we may conclude that Paul was free to have long hair, short hair, or a shaved head, depending on what he felt God was calling him to do. If he had been known as a "long-haired" man while in Corinth, the Corinthians would have picked up his reference in verse 14 to their own view, probably held lightly by Paul himself, that the "nature of things" tells us how men and women should wear their hair. Nevertheless, in this case, he turns the tables on them and uses their own world view to his advantage.

Paul concludes by conclusively undermining their strange extrapolation of the creation story by appealing himself to the "nature of things" as they would have understood it. It may be a phrase they had already used in dialogue with him to support their own self-styled practices. Or possibly they had expressed disgust at his own long hair when he was with them on the grounds that it was a disgrace? In which case, this reference would be amusing. Whatever the case, here he challenges their theology of male glory by referring to how God has created women, using language and concepts that they would understand. "Does not the very nature of things teach you that if a man has long hair, it is a disgrace to him, but that if a woman has long hair, it is her glory? For long hair is given to her instead of a covering." Shoemaker writes, "A further term calling for attention is *anti* (11:15)." This carries with it a strong sense of replacement. "Here I suggest the use of 'in place of' or 'instead of' as a translation, so as to emphasize the basic thrust of *anti* as indicating 'that one person or thing is, or is to be, replaced by another.'"[31] Man alone is not the image and glory of God, and

31. Shoemaker, "Unveiling," 62.

neither does woman derive her glory from him. Woman has been made naturally glorious by God through the gift of her hair, so she does not need a covering. To force her to cover her head, or worse, to shave it, would be to deny her her own natural glory.

No Such Custom

16 Εἰ δέ τις δοκεῖ φιλόνεικος εἶναι, ἡμεῖς τοιαύτην συνήθειαν οὐκ ἔχομεν οὐδὲ αἱ ἐκκλησίαι τοῦ θεοῦ.

Paul's final comment on the matter leaves no room for doubt that they should follow his correction on this, "If anyone wants to be contentious/divisive about this, we have no such custom—nor do the churches of God." The word τοιαύτην in verse 16 is best translated "such" or "sort of," not "other." Shoemaker writes, "The use of 'other' creates an affirmation of the practice in question, whereas the use of 'such' makes clear that the custom in question was inconsistent with the practice of the churches with which Paul was familiar."[32] In other words, if Paul really is ruling against rather than for head coverings, he is adamant that the Corinthian church is the only church adopting this nonsensical and oppressive practice, and is reminding them, as we have already noted, that if they wish to be argumentative about it, then they will find they are on their own.

An Exegetical Embarrassment

Having surveyed a range of traditional views, and having compared them with a rhetorical reading of the text, I contend that 1 Corinthians 11:2–16, when read in a traditional manner, poses what Brad Jersak has designated "an exegetical embarrassment" for the church, and this in a fourfold manner.[33] First, it is abundantly clear that the passage itself is one that commentators, without exception, claim is obscure. The total lack of consensus on the passage, and the wide range of readings clearly demonstrate that the church has been unable to "make sense" of this passage of Scripture. Second, despite recognizing the highly problematic nature of the traditional reading, commentators have persevered in offering speculative interpretations of this passage, leading either to appeals to customs regarding hair length

32. Ibid.

33. This phrase is one that Brad Jersak used in conversation on the subject.

in relation to homosexuality for men and shame for women, to reputed customs regarding head coverings for men and women in worship, or to a strange and contradictory view of creation theology. Third, a traditional reading creates for us an embarrassment in terms of Paul's own thought, both with respect to his own argumentation in the passage, which remains convoluted, and with respect to his wider theology, which he appears to contradict in this passage. Was Paul really so muddled or so hypocritical or so tyrannical? Fourth, there is a clear agreement among commentators that this passage contains within it an "apostolic ruling." If this is the case, then surely the church needs to make a decision as to what should be enforced for all churches everywhere. Apart from a few churches around the world that adhere to the practice of head coverings for women, for centuries the worldwide church has (with some exceptions) chosen to ignore Paul's apostolic ruling. That is unless, of course, Paul is ruling that there are no circumstances under which women should be forced to wear a head covering in worship, in which case, even though we have not previously understood the passage, the Spirit has led us to act correctly upon it all along.

1 Corinthians 14:33b–36

It may be that this proposal remains unconvincing for those who still wish to argue that Paul is the author of these views. There are some, as we have noted, who have heard a version of this argument before and have dismissed it. In concluding this chapter I will briefly summarize the claim made by a number of scholars in recent years that there is a similar pattern in 1 Corinthians 14:33b–36. Such scholars have explored the possibility that the derogatory view of women is not Paul's own, but that of his opponents. They have proposed, accordingly, that we should read 14:33b–36 as an example of Paul citing his opponents' views in order to refute them.[34] This, of course, is directly relevant to my proposed reading of 1 Corinthians 11:2–16.[35] In both passages we face the problem of the confusing nature of

34. These include Allison, "Let the Women Be Silent in the Churches"; Flanagan and Snyder, "Did Paul Put Down Women in 1 Cor 14:34–36?"; Manus, "The Subordination of Women in the Church: 1 Cor 14:33b–36 Reconsidered"; Odell-Scott, "In Defence of an Egalitarian Interpretation of 1 Cor 14:34–36."

35. See Fee, *First Epistle*, 704–5. Although Fee himself finds this view attractive, he is not convinced by this argument, mainly on the grounds that it cannot be reconciled with Paul's views on women in 1 Cor 11. If we read 1 Cor 11 as Paul arguing *against* head coverings, this has a hugely significant impact on how we might read 1 Cor 14:34–36, not

the construction and content of Paul's argument. Having dealt with chapter 11 in detail, I will not explore all the problems related to the passage in 14, nor all possible solutions offered, but will simply give a brief summary.

Of course, there are those who believe that Paul *does* wish to silence women, or married women, in public worship. They either attribute this view to what they believe is Paul's general view that women should be subordinate to men, that women should not teach, or that this injunction refers to a specific context in Corinth where the women are being unruly and rude and chattering through the services. It should be clear by now that I do not accept any of those explanations as adequate to explain either Paul's views here or the Corinthian situation. According to my view of Paul and his view of what is happening in Corinth, this passage would be totally discordant with his views, but entirely in line with my perspective on the bullying Corinthian men. Traditional explanations are riddled with inconsistencies when read within the Corinthian correspondence as a whole, and with Paul's other letters. Fee refers to this in his work and the possibility of a rhetorical reading. "Because of the very Jewish nature of this passage, others have argued that it does not represent Paul's point of view at all, but rather is a quotation or restatement of the view of some Corinthians who were imposing it on the community. Usually this is associated with the 'Cephas party' of 1:12. Vv. 36-38 are then viewed as Paul's own response to this imposition of 'the Law' on the church." Fee finds this point of view attractive, but too problematic, on the grounds that there is no precedent for such a long quotation "that is also full of argumentation (two explanatory 'for's); it presupposes the unlikely scenario that some in the church were forbidding women to speak—and especially that the quotation would come from the same Corinthian letter that is otherwise quite pro women." He cites 7:1-7 and 11:2-16 in support of the pro-women stance of the Corinthians.[36] Clearly, if we read 11:2-16 in the way that I have been advocating, this then has an impact on Fee's argument, endorsing his point about the letter being pro-women even further. In response to his caution of not being able to find a passage of equal length where Paul cites the Corinthians,

---

only in terms of Paul's method, but also with respect to his views on women. Fee cites the following works as presenting the rhetorical reading of 1 Cor 14:34-36: the translation by Helen Barrett Montgomery; cf. Bushnell, *God's Word*, par. 189-215; Kaiser, "Paul, Women, and the Church"; Flanagan and Snyder, "Did Paul Put Women Down in 1 Cor 14:34-36?"; Odell-Scott, "Let the Women Speak in Church: An Egalitarian Interpretation of 1 Cor 14:33b-36."

36. Fee, *First Epistle*, 704-5.

if there is another quotation of similar length (or even longer) in chapter 11, and on the basis of the Corinthians' treatment of the women in forcing them to wear head coverings to pray and prophecy, it is also entirely plausible that these same men have enforced certain rules regarding married women speaking in public.

I am proposing with Flanagan and Snyder that this is indeed another instance of Paul citing the Corinthians in order to correct them. Flanagan and Snyder first point out the problems inherent in the passage that are the types of problems that by now we should be accustomed to. Initially, they note a contradiction between Paul's approval of women praying and prophesying in chapter 11 and his prohibition here. Second, they note that there "is some textual difficulty with vv. 34–35. In a few manuscripts (Western text) they are found at the conclusion of the chapter, after verse 40. This suggests that they may have originated as a marginal note, later incorporated into the text at different places." Third, they point out that Paul argues from "the law" in verse 34 and comment, "[i]t is stunning to hear Paul arguing in this fashion from the law, Paul for whom 'the power of sin is the law' in 15:56." Finally, verse 36

> is truly puzzling, especially for those reading it in Greek or who are helped by a very precise translation. The Revised Standard Version translates it: "What! Did the word of God originate with you, or are you the *only ones* it has reached?" We have emphasised *only ones* because therein lies the difficulty. *In the original Greek it is masculine.* Paul is now talking to the men, where we would expect just the opposite. Vv. 34–35 clearly concern the women. Why doesn't the chiding of v. 36 continue to concern them? Why does it now aim at the men?[37]

One solution, as they point out, is that "because of the difficulties inherent in these verses an increasing number of commentators now view them as a post-Pauline interpolation. . . . The growing list of such exegetes is impressive. It includes C. K. Barrett, F. Cleary, H. Conzelmann, L. Cope, R. Fuller, D. Georgi, L. Keck, J. Murphy-O'Connor and C. Roetzel."[38] Their own solution is that verses 34–35 represent "a quotation from the letter which Paul is answering and that, as such, they express the mind of *the men* whom Paul chides in v. 36."[39] Based on the fact that Paul certainly does

37. Flanagan and Snyder, "Did Paul," 10.
38. Ibid.
39. Ibid., 11.

cite the Corinthians at various places in his letter, they write, "To argue from Paul's copious use of quotations in 1 Cor to *the possibility* of his doing that in 1 Cor 14:34–35 is, consequently, not difficult."[40] They concede that it is not possible to *prove* this, but believe that there are "however, various facts which bolster the possibility into a practicable theory."[41] Even Thiselton comments, "[m]any argue that vv. 34–35 represent a *Corinthian slogan or piece of Corinthian theology which Paul quotes, only to reject it.* Such a view is not farfetched, for Paul appears to do precisely this in 6:12; 7:1; 10:23; and perhaps elsewhere (e.g., 8:1–6)."[42]

As I have argued in relation to chapter 11 and head coverings, Flanagan and Snyder posit that Paul is here contesting male dominance, and that this view "takes seriously the strange and unexpected masculinity of v. 36." If "vv. 34–35 are a Corinthian expression of exclusive masculine dominance in the Church, Paul's response to the men in v. 36 makes perfect sense. It may be, then, that 1 Cor 14:34–35 is an indication, not of Paul's anti-feminism, but of his opposition to a male-dominated group in Corinth. If so, the Paul in this passage is but a further extension of the Paul of 1 Cor 11:5 and Gal 3:28."[43] This is consistent with what I have been arguing in relation to chapter 11. Could it be that in this passage, just as in 1 Corinthians 11, Paul is challenging their oppressive practices with respect to women in public worship, and warning them that if they wish to oppose him on the grounds that they believe themselves to be superior to Paul as they are more "spiritually gifted" than he, that they run the risk of falling into severe opprobrium?

---

40. Ibid.

41. Ibid.

42. Thiselton, *First Epistle*, 1150.

43. Flanagan and Snyder, "Did Paul," 12.

FIVE

The Value of Tongues and Prophecy

Introduction

Having surveyed two passages thus far, I wish now to turn to one last passage in chapter 14 concerning the unruly exercising of the gift of tongues in public worship. In this chapter, we will examine this passage, noting similar difficulties and patterns that we have already encountered in 11:2–16 and 14:33b–36. All three passages are marked by inconsistencies and contradictions within the text and, therefore, pose exegetical difficulties. As I have noted previously, I suggest that there are indeed three instances in the section on worship in chapters 11–14 where Paul carefully crafts his argument using longer references to Corinthian thought in such a way as to correct an undesirable Corinthian practice. In the case of 14:20–25, the practice in question is that of the tongues-speakers in the church speaking in tongues in public worship all at once. These verses come near the end of the section on orderly worship. Paul has corrected the Corinthians over their practice of head coverings for women, their selfish and oppressive behavior at the communion table, schism within the body, the belief that certain members were entitled to greater honor, and the exercise of spiritual gifts without loving regard to others. He has exhorted them in the strongest possible terms to love one another in a Christlike manner, articulating for them how he believes this should be lived out in concrete ways. They are one body and should avoid schism and contempt or disdain for the other at all costs. In a similar vein to my proposal, B. C. Johanson argues that the difficulties encountered in 14:20–25 might *also* be resolved by a version of a rhetorical reading.[1] In this chapter, I examine his argument, before presenting a modified version of it.

Love and Gifts

The beginning of chapter 14 encapsulates Paul's view of the exercise of all spiritual gifts, "Make love your aim, and earnestly desire spiritual gifts . . ." he goes on to add, "especially that you may prophesy" (14:1). What follows is Paul's teaching on the gift of tongues and the gift of prophecy. His summation at the end of the chapter wraps it up: "So, my brethren, earnestly desire to prophesy, and do not forbid speaking in tongues; but all things should be done decently and in order" (vv. 39–40). Despite the Corinthians' overtly unloving use of spiritual gifts, Paul continues to encourage them to seek and to use the gifts, if they will correct the manner in which they use them. Paul's response to the use of spiritual gifts is surprising: rather than putting a stop to their use altogether in this unruly congregation, Paul continues to encourage their use, as long as they are exercised in a loving and caring manner. With respect to tongues, Paul makes it clear that he still sees this gift as valuable, however, as it is primarily a gift that edifies the speaker of tongues, it is of limited value in public worship. Tongues, the language of angels, is unintelligible to the outsider or the uninitiated—the nontongues speaker. The language of tongues can be "interpreted" or given meaning for those who hear, but Paul teaches that this gift is primarily a gift of prayer that edifies the spirit. The mind is not engaged in the same way as it is when listening to words spoken in an intelligible language. Prophecy is a superior gift for two reasons. First, prophecy consists of words of edification and revelation brought to the entire church, and thus no one will be excluded on the basis that they cannot understand. As Paul's emphasis throughout the whole of Corinthians is that of unity over schism, it is entirely consonant with this view that he should restrict and/or frame the speaking of tongues in public worship so that it does not function as an exclusive practice. Tongues is potentially divisive, as it is even today, between those who have the gift of speaking in tongues and those who do not. Unbelievers will not have the gift of tongues, and neither will many believers. Prophecy, like preaching, however, is a message to the whole church. Second, and perhaps more importantly for Paul, prophecy can have a powerful effect on the outsider or unbeliever, as Paul describes at the end of the chapter.

1. Johanson, "Tongues."

From the lead in to 14:20–25, it is clear that Paul sees tongues as a valuable but secondary gift to prophecy. It has value only for the individual and for the "initiated." Paul also sees its value if those who speak in tongues can in addition receive some kind of interpretation (14:27). However, the overall message of chapter 14 is that uninterpreted tongues is of no value in terms of edification for those who are nontongues speakers, whether uninitiated but within the church or unbelievers. Paul values and appreciates the gift of tongues, but his preference is for prophecy (14:18–9). Prophecy is more "loving" of the other, whether the other is the nontongues-speaking believer or the outsider. These views, attributed to Paul, do not in themselves pose any problems and are compatible with the illustrations in verses 23–25. One of the main problems, however, is his assertion in verse 22, "[t]hus, tongues are a sign not for believers but for unbelievers, while prophecy is not for unbelievers but for believers." This verse is framed by teaching and illustrations that lead us to imagine that Paul was going to say precisely the opposite! What then do we do with this verse?

Contradictions and Ambiguities

Verses 20–25, like 11:2–16, immediately raise questions in the inquisitive reader's mind. What is Paul actually saying in verse 22 in the light of what has preceded this verse and also in the light of the illustrations that follow? As we saw in 11:2–16, anyone arguing that the whole passage reflects Paul's opinions has to attempt to fathom what Paul means and possibly to attempt to reconcile two tensive or contradictory views. The same applies here, although here the contradiction is even more marked. Paul apparently directly contradicts himself. Johanson highlights a number of problems. The main problems occur as commentators first attempt to establish the relationship of the assertions made about tongues and prophecy in verse 22 to the quotation of Isaiah 28:11–12 in verse 21 and then attempt to apply those insights to the illustrations concerning tongues and prophecy in verses 23–25, which contradict the previous assertions.[2] Having explained the value of tongues for the individual believer, and for the church in a limited sense, Paul then apparently claims that tongues are a sign for unbelievers and *not* believers and, in order to support his view, he appears to be appealing to the Isaiah passage. As Johanson notes, this raises the question of how

2. Ibid., 180.

the Isaiah quote substantiates this claim.[3] This is the first challenge. This is
further exacerbated by the fact that the Isaiah passage in question has been
adapted in this context, which we will discuss below. The second challenge
arises as the passage continues and we find that Paul gives us an illustration
of a possible scenario that implies the opposite! If the unbelievers or those
who do not understand come in, and you are all speaking in tongues, won't
they say you are out of your mind? In what sense then is tongues a "sign" for
them? The same contradiction occurs with Paul's claims about prophecy.
Having made it clear that he views prophecy as a superior gift because it
is intelligible to all, in verse 22 he claims that it is for believers and not
unbelievers, and yet he also goes on in verses 24–25 to describe a dramatic
scene in which the unbeliever comes in while all are prophesying, she is
convinced by all that she is a sinner, that she will be judged by all because
the secrets of her heart are laid bare, and so she will fall down and worship
God, exclaiming, "God is really among you!"

Most commentators attempt to reconcile the illustrations with the assertions in some way. Not all, however. As Johanson writes, there are those
who have tried to avoid the contradiction or ambiguity by manipulating
the text itself.

> W. Barclay completely omits the assertion concerning prophecy
> (v. 22b) without so much as a remark in his comments or footnote
> to signal that he has done so! On the other hand, J. B. Phillips is
> so pressed by the contradiction as to make his sole alteration of
> the text without any support whatsoever of a textual variant. This
> he does by reversing the order of the references to "believers" and
> "unbelievers" in both assertions respectively.[4]

Others do not take such drastic liberties with the text, but then must attempt to resolve the contradiction or ambiguity in the interpretation of certain key words. Discussion on the meaning of this passage thus centers on
three critical hermeneutical decisions: (1) the meaning of σημεῖον (sign),
(2) Paul's use of the Isaiah passage in an adapted form, and (3) the meaning
of ἄπιστος (unbeliever) as it is used in both the assertions and the illustrations. In what follows I will summarize how some commentators attempt
to read a coherent message out of chapter 14, and then compare it with a
rhetorical reading. We will begin with the use of the Isaiah passage.

---

3. Ibid.

4. Barclay, *The Letter to the Corinthians*, 146–47; Phillips, *The New Testament in Modern English*, 367 & 550, cited in Johanson, "Tongues," 181.

The Isaiah Text

The first issue arises out of the fact that the Isaiah quote diverges substantially from the MT and the LXX. Johanson notes, "Either it is quoted loosely or else from a Greek translation other than the LXX. . . . Origen . . . claims to have found the text of Paul's quotation in Aquila's and other Greek versions apart from the LXX."[5] Johanson notes the differences between the three versions in 1 Corinthians, the MT, and the LXX. His comparisons are below:

1 Corinthians

By men of strange tongues and by the lips of foreigners
will I speak to this people
and even then they will not listen to me, says the Lord.

MT

Nay, but by men of strange lips and with an alien tongue
the Lord will speak to this people, to whom he has said, "This is rest;
give rest to the weary; and this is repose"; yet they would not hear.

LXX

through the contemptuous speech of lips, through another tongue
for they will speak to this people,
saying to them
"This is rest for the hungry; and this is the calamity";
but they would not hear.[6]

First, with respect to the differences, Johanson writes,

> In noting the more significant changes we should point out that
> 1) Paul has "I will speak" in the place of "the Lord will speak" (MT)
> and "they will speak" (LXX); 2) he omits the intelligible message

5. See Origen, *Philocalia*, IX, 2, cited in Johanson, "Tongues," 181.
6. Johanson, "Tongues," 181–82.

spoken by the "Lord" (MT) and "they" (LXX) to which "this peo-ple" refuse to listen in both cases; and 3) he adds the authoritative phrase λέγει κύριος found neither in the MT nor in the LXX.[7]

The result is that the Corinthians version of the Isaiah passage actually de-picts a different situation from that in the MT or the LXX. The situation described in the MT is that the people will be spoken to by men of "strange tongues," the Assyrians, due to their refusal to listen to God's intelligible message previously given to them. In the LXX, as Johanson notes, "it is not clear whether it is the drunken prophets and priests (v. 7) or the foreigners who are represented as doing the speaking. In either case their message as distinct from God's message is a message of doom, while in common with God's message in the MT it is intelligible."[8] In the Corinthians text, even though God will speak "by men of unintelligible speech, 'this people' will *even then* not listen."[9] As Johanson notes, this text demonstrates that unintelligible tongues will be ineffective in causing "this people to listen to the Lord," and he goes on, "We should further note that the omission of the intelligible message [in the Corinthian extract] has the effect of making the object of the hearer's refusal to listen, not the intelligible message as in the MT and LXX, but the unintelligible speech of 'foreigners' through whom God will speak."[10] This is a substantial reworking, not only of the wording, but of the meaning of the text. C. D. Stanley concedes that "[d]etermining the precise relationship between the wording of 1 Cor 14:21 and the text of the LXX is one of the greatest challenges in the entire corpus of Pauline citations."[11]

How can we explain this unusual quotation? Some have blamed Paul's faulty memory while others appeal to the possibility that Paul had access to a translation that we no longer have,[12] and still others argue that Paul has no compunction in using scriptural quotations out of context.[13] We cannot provide a definitive answer to this question. If this is Paul, and there

7. Ibid., 182.

8. Ibid.

9. Ibid.

10. Ibid.

11. Stanley, *Paul and the Language of Scripture,* 198, cited in Thiselton, *The First Epistle,* 1120.

12. Thiselton, *The First Epistle,* 1120.

13. Johanson cites Grant, *A Short History of the Interpretation of the Bible,* 28–42, for evidence of noncontextual use of OT Scripture by Paul, in "Tongues," 183.

is no other translation that he is citing, then either he holds the quotation loosely, or he alters the text to quote a version that fits with his argument.[14] The second challenge presented to us by this text is what the relationship is between this passage and the Corinthian situation. Why would Paul cite this particular passage, and how is it applied? What is the point that he is making? Thiselton believes there is a way of leaving the text as it is written and finding a way through to construct a coherent picture of Paul's thought. He argues that it is possible to apply the verses from Isaiah to the Corinthian situation even given that the point that Paul subsequently makes regarding tongues and believers and unbelievers appears to be contradictory.

Isaiah and the Corinthians

Thiselton notes first that in the Isaiah passage in the LXX the unintelligible speech serves "as a sign of judgment, of not-belonging, for unbelief."[15] He then applies this theme to the Corinthian situation with respect to those who have the gift of tongues and those who do not, focusing on the motif of not-belonging over and above any other theme. In relation to tongues-speaking in Corinth, he writes that the effect of speaking in tongues on the nontongues speaker, whether they are believers or unbelievers, is to put them in a position that is "inappropriate or self-defeating." The non-tongues-speaking believer "may feel 'alien' even within the worshiping community." For Thiselton, there are two types of outsider in this scenario: the believing nontongues speaker who belongs but is, in effect, left out, and the non-Christian. Prophecy is effective for the latter. So he writes, "it is prophetic proclamation of the gospel, not tongues, that will bring the unbeliever who may be present to Christian faith."[16] Thiselton proposes that Paul is against any tongues-speaking in public because "it places many of God's own people in the situation of feeling like foreigners in a foreign land and 'not at home' in their own home." Secondly, it will fail to bring the message of the Christian gospel home to unbelievers.[17] Thiselton makes a number

---

14. Johanson, "Tongues," 182.

15. Ibid., 1118.

16. Ibid., 1118–19.

17. Thiselton gives a complex answer to the question of the parallels between Isaiah and Corinth. These are his reasons: "[t]his now accounts for many of the similarities to, and apparent divergences from, the LXX text of Isa 28:11–12, *for Paul is simultaneously quoting and applying the passage.* (1) The repetitive use of ἕτερος as an adjective or as

of complex moves in his reading of this passage predicated on two different meanings of "sign," two different meanings of "unbeliever," and a very loose connection between the Isaiah passage and the Corinthian situation.

One difficulty with Thiselton's hypothesis here is the disjunction between the situation described in Isaiah and the one at Corinth. The reason he posits for feeling alien and not at home in amongst a tongues-speaking throng is a different reason from the alienation of God's people described in Isaiah. In Isaiah, it is due to the hardness of heart among the people of God that they are subjected to a sign of judgment in the foreign tongue of the Assyrians, as Thiselton himself acknowledges.[18] They are subjected to a message that they cannot understand because of their unbelief, but this is due to their own refusal to listen to God's voice, not because of the unintelligibility of the tongue. In Corinth, it is not the nontongues-speaking Christians who are at fault, nor is it the unbelievers. It is the tongues speakers who are exercising their gift thoughtlessly and possibly in a way that they believe puts them in a superior position. Thiselton's proposal is based on a very tenuous thematic link. However, if we do choose to agree with Thiselton's unifying theme of "not-belonging" we still need to explain in what manner tongues is a "sign" and who the unbelievers and outsiders are.

Tongues—A Σημεῖον for Unbelievers

In order to describe this passage as a coherent whole, commentators must follow complex trains of thought in relation to this word σημεῖον. It should be noted that Paul does not actually reiterate the word σημεῖον in relation to prophecy in verse 22, but commentators are agreed that the sense of the text is that he is saying that prophecy also acts as a "sign" in some way, hence the debate about the use of the word in relation to both tongues and prophecy. Trevor Peterson has provided a survey and a short summary of the different interpretations of "sign" and how it might be understood in

---

part of a compound faithfully conveys the force of 28:11, but resonates with the wordplay between disdain for 'the other' and concern for 'the other'. . . . (2) The use of the first person λαλήσω is intensified by perceiving the prophet or apostle in a context of divine agency by the addition of . . . λέγει κύριος. (3) Some aspects of 28:11 do not directly apply to the situation, and parts of the quotations are often omitted. (4) The future tense embraces the consequences which will follow if people persist in their love of the esoteric or unusual at the expense of the welfare of 'the other,' for whom Christ died (cf. 8:6–13)." *The First Epistle*, 1121–22.

18. Ibid., 1123.

ways that will then make sense of the Isaiah quotation and the illustration.[19] The first is that tongues are a sign of judgment on unbelievers, functioning in a similar way to the parables of Jesus, in that they shroud meaning so that those who refuse to receive God's message cannot in fact do so.[20]

The second is that tongues are a sign that actively produce unbelief, "not only confirming unbelief, but producing still more unbelief and hardening." Peterson quotes C. R. Erdman, who writes of the "'melancholy purpose for those who were rejecting the simple gospel of Christ,' suggesting that it 'confirmed them and made them feel justified in their unbelief,' as well as provoking them to insult the church and its people."[21]

Third is tongues as a sign of God's grace to unbelievers.

> F. W. Grosheide takes Isaiah's prophecy as hypothetical, suggesting that "the judgment upon Israel was that it, after it had heard the voice of the Lord, delivered by the prophets, would not listen even if the Lord spoke through foreign nations." He goes on to call the sign "a new token of His grace thereby to arouse the attention of the people." In the same way, tongues today and in Paul's time serve to point the way to salvation—a sign which believers do not need to see but which unbelievers might receive.[22]

The fourth interpretation is tongues as a pagan sign.

> P. Roberts suggests that a more consistent view begins with understanding that, as a sign to unbelievers, tongues would have to be readily recognizable to pagans as an indicator of divine activity. Paul's accusation against the Corinthians, then, is that they are looking for the sort of indistinct sign that a pagan would seek, rather than maturing to the point at which a Christian should recognize less ecstatic indicators. Roberts sees no more relevance in the Isaiah prophecy than that it deals with the ineffectiveness of strange tongues.[23]

---

19. Peterson, "The Use of Isa 28:11–12 in 1 Cor 14:20–22."

20. See Robertson and Plummer, *A Critical and Exegetical Commentary,* 316, cited in Peterson, "The Use of Isa," 2.

21. Peterson, "The Use of Isa," 2–3. Peterson cites Erdman, *The First Epistle of Paul,* 146.

22. Grosheide, *Commentary on the First Epistle,* 330–31, cited in Peterson, "The Use of Isa," 3.

23. Roberts, "A Sign—Christian or Pagan?", 200–201, cited in Peterson, "The Use of Isa," 3–4.

Thiselton marries the Isaiah situation to the Corinthian situation through the motifs of the outsider, judgment, belonging, and belief in relation to Paul's use of the word σημεῖον. The fact that this passage deals with all those motifs is certainly true, but are the connections really so clear? And how then do we reconcile Paul's first statement regarding unbelievers and believers to his illustrations? Thiselton posits that despite tongues being a gift from God, it is possible for tongues to function as a negative sign illuminating the unbelief of unbelievers, but at the same time powerless to convict them of sin and draw them to faith. If tongues is exercised in the wrong way, as it is in Corinth, it only serves to alienate an unbeliever or a nontongues speaker by confirming skepticism instead of arousing and inspiring faith and should not, therefore, be part of the community of worship.[24] This is compatible with the illustrations. If we accept this, however, we then have to explain how prophecy functions as a "sign," but in a different way so as to engender a positive outcome. There are a number of commentators who follow this line of thinking, that tongues is a "sign" with an overall negative impact on the unbeliever, unlike prophecy, which has a positive impact on the unbeliever, drawing him or her to faith in God. Thiselton summarizes these perspectives: "Grudem concludes that tongues without interpretation are a sign to unbelievers of God's judgment and displeasure, whereas prophecy ministers to the experience of God's presence and blessing."[25] "Lanier similarly argues that Paul follows on logically from the condemnatory force of Isa 28:11–12 to argue for the judgmental significance and hence the damning effect of tongues upon those who are unbelievers."[26] And Thiselton himself, "Paul portrays speaking in tongues as a sign which inexpert unbelievers (rightly or wrongly) associate with, and interpret as, pagan μανιά, and thereby are pushed yet further away into judgment. On the other hand, prophetic speech brings genuine conviction . . . of truth, and hence faith."[27] In Thiselton's view the judgment that comes on the unbeliever through prophecy is, in contrast, entirely positive. On hearing the prophetic word, the unbeliever "undergoes conviction and

---

24. Thiselton, *The First Epistle*, 1122–23.

25. Grudem, "1 Cor 14:20–25," 381–96, cited in Thiselton, *The First Epistle*, 1125.

26. Lanier, "With Stammering Lips and Another Tongue," 259–85, cited in Thiselton, *The First Epistle*, 1125–26.

27. Thiselton, *The First Epistle*, 1126.

judgment . . . the words of the prophets bring home the truth of the gospel in such a way that the hearer 'stands under' the verdict of the cross."[28]

Thiselton's position can be summarized in the following way:

1. Paul states that the experience of being surrounded by the "tongues" of the Assyrians served as a sign that Israel had been placed under God's judgment for unbelief.

2. This was an inappropriate situation for the people of God, "who had been misled by the 'people of influence' who expressed skepticism about Isaiah's message."

3. "Hence Christian believers should not have such a 'sign' marking their community worship and thereby generating a sense of 'wrongness' or 'strangeness' more appropriate to what *unbelievers* might be expected to feel."

4. Conversely, prophetic speech signals "the presence and action of God in nurturing people of faith."

5. "Hence on one side prophetic speech characterizes the believing church at worship; tongues, on the other side, constitute negative signs (at least in public and in their effect) generating barriers and alienation inappropriate for believers."[29]

His argument rests on "sign" being used in one way with respect to unbelievers and tongues and in another way with respect to prophecy. "Our translation therefore is designed to indicate that εἰς σημεῖον carries a different force in each of its different contexts."[30]

In summary, the "two types of sign" theory posits that tongues are a negative "sign" for unbelievers and/or nontongues-speaking believers, pushing them further away into judgment or alienation, whereas prophecy is a means of grace. None of this is actually explained by the text itself. We are left to infer such a reading from a connection with a "loose" reading of an emended OT text, and an imagined use of the concept of a "sign" in two opposite ways (negative and positive) in relation first to tongues and then to prophecy, in order to harmonize verse 22 with the illustrations and the preceding teaching.

28. Ibid., 1128.
29. Ibid., 1123.
30. Ibid.

Another solution is to read "sign" as negative in both cases, which has the advantage of greater consistency in the first instance, but then creates problems later in relation to the illustrations, where prophecy has an over-whelmingly positive function and effect. Barrett suggests that Paul refers to the Isaiah passage because

> it is probably the word "men of other tongues" that caught his eye and suggested the application of the passage to his discussion of "tongues." It is this, rather than the historical setting of the proph-ecy, in which Isaiah threatens his people, who have failed to listen to his words, with the foreign speech of Assyrian invaders, that is in Paul's mind.[31]

In Barrett's view "sign" is thoroughly negative, even in relation to prophecy. He writes, "prophecy acts upon the Corinthian believers in the same way that tongues act upon 'outsiders.' The Corinthians tend to shut their ears to prophecy because they gain more satisfaction from listening to tongues than from hearing their faults exposed and their duties pointed out in plain rational language. Thus they incur judgment."[32] This reading relies on a very loose connection in Paul's mind in employing the Isaiah pas-sage to make a point, and leaves us in some confusion in relating verse 22 directly to the illustrations. It is now clear that we cannot make a decision as to how we will interpret the word "sign" without making a corresponding decision about Paul's use of "unbeliever" and "believer."

Having surveyed examples of how we might interpret the idea of tongues as a "sign" for unbelievers or outsiders if we believe that this is all the voice of Paul, the reader must make a decision as to which is more plausible. However, if we do wish to attempt to hold the passage together as Paul's view, we are forced to articulate a particular understanding of the word σημεῖον in relation to tongues in verse 22 (in order to make sense of the illustrations in verses 23–24) and then in another, contradictory sense in relation to prophecy, unless we go on to argue that he uses "believer" and "unbeliever" in one sense in the assertions and then in a different sense in the illustrations. If we wish to argue that he uses the word "sign" univocally with regard to both tongues and prophecy this will then cause problems in relating verse 22 to the illustrations, which can only be resolved by argu-ing that he must be using "unbeliever" in one way in verse 22 and then in another way in the illustrations, designating two different categories of

31. Barrett, *A Commentary*, 322–23.
32. Ibid., 324.

people, thus letting him and us off the hook of confusion. Who then are the unbelievers and the outsiders?

Who is the Unbeliever?

Johanson notes the complex argumentation that occurs once we have decided that tongues will be a negative sign for unbelievers. Are there two types of "unbeliever" here—one who is stubbornly unbelieving and one who is ignorantly unbelieving—or is Paul using the word univocally throughout? If the unbeliever in verse 22 is stubbornly unbelieving, then to whom is the term ἄπιστος ascribed in verses 23–25? Is Paul using the term in one way in verse 23 and another way in verses 24–25? As we have seen, Thiselton explains this by making only a loose connection between the Isaiah passage and the unbelievers and outsiders in the Corinthian church. The issue is whether the unbelievers are those who have heard the intelligible message of God and hardened their hearts or those who have not yet heard, and so do not yet believe. If we take it to mean the former, we may be able to explain away the Isaiah passage and verses 22–23, but this does not accord with the illustrations in verses 24–25. As Johanson points out, "the context of vv. 24–25 seems to indicate that the ἄπιστος refers to the non-Christian in the neutral sense."[33] Arguing that "unbeliever" is used by Paul in the same passage in different ways causes considerable confusion. Johanson quotes Robertson and Plummer as an example of those who defend different definitions of unbeliever and so explain the resulting contradiction between the second assertion (v. 22b) and the second illustration (vv. 24–25) as being only apparent.

> The explanation given is that whereas the context of the quotation shows that the ἄπιστοι in v. 22 have heard the intelligible message of God and rejected it, the ἄπιστος in vv. 24–25, as shown by the context there, has not previously heard. But only a few lines further on they seem to contradict themselves in commenting on the confession of the ἄπιστος in v. 25 that "God is really among you." They write that "in spite of his [the unbeliever] *previous scoffs and denials*, there is the Real Presence of the true God."[34]

---

33. Johanson, "Tongues," 183.

34. Robertson and Plummer, *A Critical and Exegetical Commentary*, cited in Johanson, "Tongues," 183 (my italics).

Is the unbeliever the hardhearted who has heard the intelligible message of God and rejected it, the one who has not heard, or the one who hears and receives the powerful revelation of God with a declaration of faith?

The Unbeliever: A Summary

Is it plausible that Paul uses key terms in different senses throughout the passage? It is quite clear that taken as a whole, verses 21–25 are concerned with the relation of tongues to unbelievers in contrast to the relation of prophecy to unbelievers.[35] For this reason, it is crucial that we establish who these unbelievers are, but as Johanson notes, "to use a key term in assertions with a different sense from the same term in supporting illustrations does not make sense, especially when they are so closely juxtaposed to each other. It would only be confusing and serve to weaken his argument."[36]

Johanson himself offers a detailed structural analysis of the passage "on the literary and argumentative levels," examining the parallelisms in verses 20–25 and the lexical and exegetical issues in the passage in relation to Paul's argumentation.[37] As well as exposing the weaknesses in the arguments in favor of a Pauline voice throughout, he forms a strong argument for this being another instance of Paul engaging with a Corinthian perspective. He notes the strikingly abundant use of antithetical parallelism (vv. 20, 22, 23–25), which drives home his point that Paul is comparing tongues to prophecy in relation to those who hear, and not using key terms in different senses in a way that requires a significant amount of guesswork from the reader. "This parallelism is further strengthened when we note that on both sides and in each case the ἄπιστοι are included among the hearers."[38] So as a result of the parallelisms that he identifies, he writes, "I would hold that it is highly unlikely that ἄπιστος may be taken in any other than one uniform sense throughout."[39] He adds, "Taking our clue from vv. 24–25, where ἄπιστος rather clearly refers to an unbeliever without any stigma of disbelief attached, I suggest that this is the meaning which should be taken in the other three occurrences in vv. 22–23."[40] Johanson's argument is that

35. Johanson, "Tongues," 188.
36. Ibid., 183–84.
37. Ibid., 186.
38. Ibid., 187.
39. Ibid., 188.
40. Ibid., 188–89.

the parallelisms "bind the quotation, the assertions and the illustrations to-gether" while also bringing out the "highly rhetorical style of the passage," which he argues is typical of diatribe.[41]

B. C. Johanson's Rhetorical Argument

Despite admirable attempts to bring coherence to this argument, it is hard not to sympathize with Hays, who states that he finds Paul's argument here "somewhat garbled."[42] It is clear that if we assign the entire text to Paul, some sort of proposed manipulation must be accepted based on a consid-erable amount of guesswork as to the manner of equivocation that Paul is presenting in this short passage. As Johanson notes, "no matter how one takes σημεῖον, some sort of manipulation of the text, of the term ἄπιστος, or explaining away of a phrase seems unavoidable." Having clearly dem-onstrated the considerable difficulties of the traditional readings of this passage, Johanson himself offers a rhetorical reading of the text. However, he does not go so far as to postulate that Paul might be directly citing a Corinthian maxim or parroting a Corinthian phrase. Rather, he argues that Paul is referring to a Corinthian idea. I concur with Johanson's assessment of the situation, that Paul is addressing his argument for an unambiguous reading of "unbeliever," and for a positive rather than a negative reading of "sign." I depart from his reading slightly in seeing more than just a vague possibility that Paul is citing his opponents more directly, but we will come to this below.

Johanson rightly asserts that Paul here is targeting the glossolalists' childish thinking. Johanson proposes that Paul is targeting an opponent who is "arguing for the authenticating, apologetic sign value of tongues for non-Christians as opposed to Christians, while limiting the same sign value of prophecy to the church."[43] This is the key issue. "According to our proposed solution, this claim for the apologetic value of tongues clearly becomes *the* bone of contention in 1 Cor. xiv. 20–5."[44] As he notes, once the assertions in verse 22 are taken to reflect Paul's own views, most commen-tators then reject "the positive sense for σημεῖον due to the obvious contra-dictions resulting between the assertions and the illustrations. Instead they

41. Ibid., 189–90.
42. Hays, *First Corinthians*, 239–40.
43. Johanson, "Tongues," 194.
44. Ibid.

have accepted the negative sense and then set about trying to clear up the ambiguities."[45] If, on the other hand, we understand σημεῖον in a positive sense, we would then need to "attribute the assertions in v. 22 to someone other than Paul." He works from this premise to propose a new solution.

His first move is to read verse 22 as a Pauline rhetorical question: are tongues, then, meant as a sign not for believers but for unbelievers, while prophecy is meant as a sign not for unbelievers but for believers? Johanson argues that this reading may be made argumentatively feasible in two ways. The first, he concedes, is that there is "a remote possibility that Paul may be quoting a slogan of the glossolalists in v. 22 which they possibly developed by inference from Isa. xxviii. 11–12." He rejects this, however, arguing that it "seems more likely . . . that Paul, being informed of the glossolalists' views, quotes Isa. xxviii. 11–12 (which may or may not have been known to them), and then proceeds to place their views in the mouth of an imaginary opponent as an inference drawn from the quotation."[46] He goes on to note that "the λαός in v. 21 may be taken to refer to the πιστεύοντες in v. 22a, i.e., the Christian community, the inference being drawn that since tongues have been shown to be ineffective in the church they must then be meant as an authenticating, apologetic sign 'not for believers but for unbelievers,' i.e., non-Christians."[47]

Johanson argues that Paul is writing "informed by the childish thinking of the Corinthian glossolalists" in verses 20–22 and thus "extends the inference to say that prophecy is meant as a positive sign 'not for unbelievers but for believers.'"[48] Johanson sees the rebuttal coming in verses 23–25, where Paul shows

> that for the non-Christian tongues are madness, while it is rather prophecy that convicts his heart and convinces him of God's presence among the believers. On this view the ambiguity between the quotation and the assertions occasioned by the contradictions of the illustrations . . . is taken away, the uniform sense of repeated key terms like ἄπιστος as required by the literary structure is upheld, and the argument is demonstrated to move meaningfully with the characteristic force and brevity of a diatribe.[49]

45. Ibid., 188.
46. Ibid., 193.
47. Ibid., 193–94.
48. Ibid., 194.
49. Ibid.

He summarizes his argument as verses 21–25 containing Paul's rebuke of the Corinthian glossolalists for their immature thinking. In his view, Paul introduces the quote from Isaiah in order to use the text "as a springboard for the following assertions in v. 22. These assertions are *taken to reflect the content of the glossolalists' childish thought*. Paul places them in the mouth of an imaginary opponent as being drawn from inference from the quotation, and casts them in the form of a rhetorical question."[50] He thus argues that Paul's opponent "is arguing for the authenticating, apologetic sign value of tongues for non-Christians as opposed to Christians, while limiting the same sign value of prophecy to the church."[51] Paul makes it clear that non-Christians visiting the church would think that the tongues-speakers were all mad, whereas prophecy would have a powerful effect in bringing God's revelation to the non-Christian in a personal and specific way.

Interestingly, Thiselton admits that Johanson's work does have the merit of "consistency and plausibility." At the same time, however, he rejects it and sticks to his point regarding the alienating effect of tongues-speaking on nontongues-speaking Christians. "In our view, Paul's appeal to the experience of making those who do not share glossolalia feel 'alien' among aliens, like the exiled to whom Isaiah refers, provides sufficient explanation of v. 21 without resort to Johanson's hypothesis."[52] Having said this, a few paragraphs further on in his argument, he returns to Johanson in what appears to be a moment of vacillation, musing, "we may concede with Johanson that if all else fails, we must take seriously the possibility of the use of a Corinthian maxim."[53] The question for the reader of 1 Corinthians is this: at what point do we make a decision that all else might have "failed"?

A Rhetorical Pattern

What is discernible in 11:2–16, 14:20–25 and 14:34–36 is a rhetorical pattern that, if read in a particular way, resolves the textual, exegetical, and theological contradictions that arise from all of these passages. I am proposing that in all these passages Paul is citing phrases from the Corinthian letter. In the tongues passage I propose that this begins at verse 21, "In the law it is written . . ." followed by the Corinthian citation of the Isaiah

50. Ibid. (my italics).

51. Ibid.

52. Thiselton, *The First Epistle*, 1124.

53. Ibid., 1126.

text, which they use to justify tongues-speaking as having some kind of apologetic sign value for non-Christians. Thus, following Johanson, I posit that the Corinthians viewed the value of the tongues for unbelievers and outsiders to consist in the outsiders witnessing the impressive display of charismata, causing them to confess "God is among you."[54] At the same time, the manifestation endorses the glossolalists' elevated spiritual status. It is perfectly plausible that the domineering group of tongues-speakers have persuaded the congregation that speaking in tongues has a particular spiritual power and significance, and therefore has value for non-Christians, even though they cannot "understand" what is going on. God is "speaking" through the tongues which, after all, is the language of angels. The fact that it is not "understood" is not the responsibility of the Corinthians, as there is a long tradition of God "speaking" and not being heard. Thus my proposed scenario is that the "spiritual ones" were using tongues as an authenticating badge of their superior and angelic status and claiming that God was 'speaking' through them, despite the fact that what they were saying was unintelligible. They did not particularly care that what they were saying was unintelligible to nontongues speakers and unbelievers because, in their view, tongues could still function as a positive, impressive "sign" of God's presence and glory. They support this practice and thinking by their manipulated version of Isaiah, which they have previously cited to Paul. Thus tongues are a "sign" for unbelievers.[55] I propose also then that the Corinthians were viewing prophecy as the revelation of the mysteries of God, and knowledge intended only for the insiders and the initiated. It had become an in-house practice for those already "in the know." This view of the use of tongues and prophecy makes sense of the passage and accords with what we know of the Corinthian church. They are rebuked by Paul for their elitism and exclusivism, their factions, their pride in their spiritual gifts, and their distorted view of their own angelic status, all of which is anathema to him.

If the Corinthians had written to Paul defending their practice by citing "the law," giving the reference and then claiming, "[t]hus tongues are a sign not for believers but for unbelievers, while prophecy is not for unbelievers but for believers," then what frames this citation is Paul's own views: don't be children, but be mature—if the whole church assembles and

---

54. Johanson, "Tongues," 200.

55. As well as drawing on Johanson's views, I owe part of this explanation to Justin Stratis, who suggested this in conversation.

all speak in tongues, and outsiders or unbelievers enter, will they not say that you are out of your mind? Note that Paul's response comes in the form of a rhetorical question, the like of which we have seen in 11:13 and will see again in 14:36. Prophecy, on the other hand, might have a powerful effect on an unbeliever—the secrets of her heart will be laid bare, she will fall on her face in worship declaring that God is really among you. All that has preceded this passage in chapter 14 supports these views as belonging to Paul. Verses 21–22 are an interruption of another voice defending a particular practice that Paul is attempting to expose as immature, selfish, and indefensible in relation to outsiders.

Paul carries on advising them that messages in tongues and prophetic words may be brought by individuals one at a time, interpreted, weighed, and tested. If revelation comes to the next person, the first person must yield to that person and allow them to speak. The picture that Paul paints is of spiritual gifts being exercised among the entire congregation, with a kind of communal and internal regulation: "For you can all prophesy one by one, so that all may learn and all be encouraged; and the spirits of the prophets are subject to prophets" (v. 31). There is no hint in these verses that this only applies to the men. In fact, even those who believe that Paul wishes women to have their heads covered must concede that he is happy to have them prophesy. We have also already noted that he describes the gift of prophecy as being that which edifies the whole church and that he elevates the gift of prophecy above the gift of teaching. His use of first, second, and third in 1 Corinthians 12:28 expresses priority and precedence in relation to apostles, prophets, and teachers. Women, therefore, take part in a gift that he views as having priority over teaching. It seems almost ludicrous in the light of this that he would also attempt to implement a contradictory practice that women should stay silent. "As in all the churches of the saints, the women should keep silence in the churches. For they are not permitted to speak, but should be subordinate, as even the law says." From verse 35 it sounds as if Paul might be addressing only the married women, "If there is anything they desire to know, let them ask their husbands at home. For it is shameful for a woman to speak in church." What if, however, rather than the married women chattering and behaving in an unruly fashion, or Paul wishing to suppress the women's voices, the dominant and gifted Corinthian men are implementing "rules" designed to subordinate the women? The formula in this passage is the same as in 14:21—"the law says," only in this instance it is difficult to ascertain which law and where. It may be that the Corinthians have found something written down to which they appeal. The married women in Corinth are being told they are not to question (or possibly challenge?) what the men are teaching. Why? Because the men are teaching the subordination of woman to man, and the derivation of woman from man, as we have seen in chapter 11. Just as in 14:23, Paul responds to their faulty thinking with a rhetorical question. "What! Did the word of God originate with you, or are you the only ones it has reached?" The Corinthian men are absolutely not to lay down "the law," and a questionable law at that, in order to keep women quiet. Paul delivers a final rebuke in 14:37–38 that is entirely reminiscent of 11:16 where he warns them not to be contentious for fear of being isolated, "If any one thinks that he is a prophet, or spiritual, he should acknowledge that what I am writing to you is a command of the Lord. If any one does not recognize this, he is not recognized" (RSV).

Paul in Context

Paul: Misogynist or Radical?

Of course it will be argued that nobody can *prove* that Paul is arguing against oppressive, bullying, and childish Corinthian practices in 1 Corinthians 11–14. This is true. I have argued that in our readings of Paul, much depends on who we believe Paul to be. Was Paul a misogynist? Was he just committed to a gentle patriarchy? Was he confused? Or was he a radical? Our prior conceptions of him will clearly affect our reading of his letters. Lakey argues that Paul was a committed subordinationist. Payne, on the other hand, argues that Paul was a radical when it came to women. He refers to the fact that Paul was educated in a countercultural way and influenced by his teacher Gamaliel. "Gamaliel's affirmations of woman pave the way for *Midr. Rab. Exod.* 14, 15: 'Before God all are equal: women and slaves, poor and rich'; and *Tanna Elialm R.* 9: 'Whether Israelite or Gentile, man or woman, male or female slave—according to their works the Holy Spirit dwells also upon him.'"[1] Payne quite rightly emphasizes Paul's unusual elevation of women. He also emphasizes the significance of Colossians 3:10 and 2 Corinthians 3:18, that all believers are being renewed in knowledge in the image of their creator.[2] Moreover, he notes that in "Col 2:10–11, Paul affirms that all Christians, female as well as male, 'have this fullness of the Godhead in Christ . . . in whom you were also circumcised.' Paul depicts females as having the fullness of the Godhead and being 'circumcised,' and he depicts males as members of the bride of Christ (Eph 5:22–27) because

---

1. Payne, *Man and Woman*, 37.
2. Ibid., 69.

their gender is irrelevant to their being in the image of God and their being in Christ."[3] Further to this, Payne goes on to comment on Ephesians 2:14, not only in relation to Jew and Gentile, but also to man and woman.

> Christ "has made the two one and has destroyed the barrier, the dividing wall of hostility" between Jew and Gentile. The court of the women with its own dividing wall lay between the court of the Gentiles and the temple. Galatians 3:28 implies the spiritual abolition of both of these walls and the consequent opening of temple-fellowship status to women as well as Gentiles. Similarly, the abolition of the necessity of circumcision (e.g., Eph 2:11–13) opens the door to full participation by women as well as Gentiles in Christian worship.[4]

Unity and Justice in Worship

What I am attempting to demonstrate in this book is that if we take a traditional view of the passages in question then it is difficult to avoid either an offensive theology of gender, or the conclusion that Paul is confused at times and double-minded at others. I have opted for a reading of Paul that avoids either of these conclusions because I believe the weight of evidence against these views is compelling. In my reading of the tongues passage, I argue for a coherent reading that avoids manipulating the text in order to bring some kind of order from what appears chaotic. The meaning of the text then becomes consistent with the surrounding teaching of Paul on tongues and prophecy. In relation to the passages on women, my starting point would be similar to Payne's who, in my opinion, is correct in his reading of Paul's relation to women. This is consistent with Campbell's reading of Galatians 3:28, and Wright's reading of Philemon. What can be claimed for the radically new relations of Jew and Gentile and slave and free can, *mutatis mutandis*, be claimed for man and woman. The status of being "in Christ' or 'in the Lord" shapes a new worshipping humanity where all come together as one before God. I would, therefore, with Wright, interpret Paul's understanding of *koinonia* as an ethical challenge. This is most clearly evident in his rebuke to the Corinthians over the Lord's Supper. It is a meal where the poor and hungry must go first, and not where the rich should lord it over those who are needy. Reading 1 Corinthians 11–14 with three instances of this style

3. Ibid.

4. Ibid., 93.

of argumentation, where Paul presents the faulty Corinthian argument followed by his corrective in the form of a question, and then a strong rebuke, reveals a great sense of harmony and coherence in this section, as well as demonstrating how it fits in with the letter as a whole. Not only does it rescue Paul either from gross misogyny or just strange and contradictory thinking, but it also gives us the key to understanding how 1 Corinthians 11–14 is entirely consistent with Paul's theology, with his views on the mutuality of relations between men and women expressed elsewhere, with his concern to look after the poor and the marginalized, and with his desire that all should be done decently and in order, which for Paul means with due consideration and care for the entire congregation.

Paul addresses a number of problems in the public worship. The first is that women are being made to veil when praying or prophesying, and being made to do so in a coercive manner. The second is that the men that Paul is addressing are behaving selfishly and greedily at the Lord's Supper. The third is that the Corinthians (or some of them) are exercising spiritual gifts in an unloving and unhelpful way, possibly preventing others from taking part in bringing prophetic words, hymns, and revelations to the gathering, acting independently, or ignoring some parts of the body. The fourth is that the "spiritual" tongues speakers have implemented a strange practice of babbling in tongues all at once on the grounds that this is a powerful witness to unbelievers. The fifth is that they are subjecting married women to remaining silent. We know that he thought that their meetings were doing more harm than good. The section on worship includes at its heart 1 Corinthians 12:31b—13:13, in which Paul describes the "more excellent way," the way of love, which must underpin all Christian worship and life together lest the church become a discordant and harsh noise to those around it. It begins and ends with two passages on the treatment of women in public worship. Traditionally, these have been read as Paul endorsing some sort of repressive or constraining practices in relation to women for the sake of propriety. I contend, however, that he is saying the opposite, and freeing women from these very practices. If this is true then, interestingly, Paul begins and ends his section on public worship by addressing the oppression of women, and coming out as strongly as possible against it.

This is in the context though of a wider picture of equality, justice, and caring for the least. All (men and women, rich and poor, Jew and Gentile) should be allowed to prophesy, as long as it is done decently and in order; all should acknowledge that everyone is needed and appreciated in the body of Christ; all spiritual gifts should be exercised within the primary ethic of love and preference for one another. Paul's rebuke over the unthinking and arrogant use of tongues is consistent with his rebuke over the treatment of women. Tongues has become a divisive weapon, used as a stamp of spirituality, rather than a loving gift used to build up the body. Paul warns them that if they speak unintelligible words they will be like foreigners to the ones who hear them (1 Cor 14:11). This defeats the purpose of the Christian community. He is totally uncompromising with the puffed-up Corinthian men who are convinced that they are right on the grounds that they hear from God and are more spiritually gifted than Paul. They are rich, reigning, and boastful, whereas Paul and his companions were a dishonored spectacle to men and angels (1 Cor 4:8–13). Paul responds, "If anybody thinks he is a prophet or spiritually gifted, let him acknowledge that what I am writing to you is the Lord's command. If he ignores this, he himself will be ignored." Paul pulls his apostolic weight in this matter.

The Cruciform Shape of Church

Paul sees Jew and Gentile, slave and free, man and woman as having been given a new identity in the crucified Christ and the baptism of the Spirit. Paul's eschatological vision is not just for some future time when Christ will return and all will be well, but has concrete and radical implications for the here and now. What emerges in a rhetorical reading of 11–14 is the consistent picture of Paul's view of Christian worship in which we give space to one another to participate and to bring gifts, giving preference to one another as we do. In sum, Paul is making a passionate plea to this group in Corinth to behave in a Christlike manner, in the way that he himself consistently did in their presence. Apostolic leadership is cruciform (1 Cor 4). It prefers others. It is characterized by Christlike love. It is sacrificial, patient, and kind. It does not envy, it is not proud. It is not rude and self-seeking. It always protects, always trusts, always hopes, always perseveres. Paul himself embodies this love. Love, respect, and honor for the other is indeed at the heart of this letter. What if the way in which Paul works this out is in the freeing of women and the poor to participate in a full and integrated manner in the worship? The barriers denoting privilege, giftedness, or proximity to God are erased. This puts 1 Corinthians 13 in a different light.

As I noted in the beginning, reading Paul will never be an easy task. We have demonstrated that his letters do indeed contain challenges for any reader, be they the scholar, the lay Christian, or the outsider to the Christian faith. We also noted that the questions surrounding Paul's views on women, and particularly in relation to the place that women occupy in the church and in worship services, are the source of much controversy. The exegesis of certain passages in Paul touches theological, ecclesial, and pastoral concerns. These matters concern how we live our lives together, what our relationships look like, who our leaders and ministers are, and how they behave. There are very few men and women in churches around the world who are not aware of this. These matters take us into questions of authority and power, who exercises power over whom, and how it is implemented. If I am correct in reading Paul in this way, this will call into question the use of the language of "covering" in general, but especially when used as a metaphorical concept to imply that a woman should have a man in authority "over" her. It is my contention that Paul's theology calls this into question anyway, especially his view of marriage in 1 Corinthians 7, and his picture of unity in Ephesians 2 and Galatians 3. His letters to the Corinthians are directly concerned with issues of authority, power, discernment, wisdom, self-sacrifice, and what it means to be identified with the crucified Christ. As I noted at the beginning, a rhetorical reading of these passages cannot be proven beyond a shadow of doubt, and can only be pieced together by "clues." I contend, however, that these clues are highly compelling and should be considered again.

The Texts

I am proposing that the words in block quotes and italics represent Corinthian thinking and phraseology. I have added some punctuation in the first section to give an indication of Paul's expression or "tone of voice," and have combined different translations rather than relying solely on one version of Scripture.

1 Corinthians 11:2–16

I praise you for remembering me in everything and for holding to the traditions/teachings, just as I passed them on to you. But I want you to realize that the head of every man is Christ, and the head of the woman is man, but the head of Christ is God.

> *Every man who prays or prophesies with his head covered dishonors his head. And every woman who prays or prophesies with her head uncovered dishonors her head—it is just as though her head were shaved.*

So if a woman does not cover her head, she should have her hair cut off; and if it is a disgrace for a woman to have her hair cut or shaved off, she should cover her head!

> *A man ought not to cover his head, since he is the image and glory of God; but the woman is the glory of man. For man did not come from woman, but woman from man; neither was man created for*

woman, but woman for man. For this reason, and because of the
angels, the woman ought to have a sign of authority on her head.

Nevertheless, [the point is] in the Lord, woman is not independent of/separated from man, nor is man independent of/separated from woman. For as woman came from man, so also man is born of woman. But everything comes from God. Judge for yourselves: Is it fitting for a woman to pray to God with her head uncovered? Does not *the very nature of things teach you that if a man has long hair, it is a disgrace to him,* but that if a woman has long hair, it is her glory? For long hair is given to her in place of a head covering. If anyone wants to be dangerously divisive about this, we have no such custom—nor do the churches of God.

1 Corinthians 14:20–25

On why tongues are a sign for believers and prophecy for unbelievers, and why the Corinthians should not elevate the gift of tongues over the gift of prophecy or speak in tongues all at once. The practice of speaking in tongues all at once without any interpretation will not bedazzle or impress unbelievers as a manifestation of God's presence, and is not justifiable from a passage in Isaiah. Tongues must be interpreted into a language that can be understood by everyone in order to be useful and to edify the church. If it is not, it is at best useless in public worship, and at worst, detrimental, as the outsiders will say that the people in the church are out of their minds.

Brothers, stop thinking like children. In regard to evil be infants, but in your thinking be adults.

In the Law it is written:

"Through men of strange tongues
and through the lips of foreigners
I will speak to this people,
but even then they will not listen to me,"
says the Lord.

Tongues, then, are a sign not for believers but for unbelievers; prophecy, however, is for believers, not for unbelievers.

So if the whole church comes together and everyone speaks in tongues, and some who do not understand or some unbelievers come in, will they not say that you are out of your mind? But if an unbeliever or someone who does not understand comes in while everybody is prophesying, he will be convinced by all that he is a sinner and will be judged by all, and the secrets of his heart will be laid bare. So he will fall down and worship God, exclaiming, "God is really among you!"

1 Corinthians 14:26–39

On who should speak in the times of worship, when and how it should be done, and how the congregation should handle prophetic words. These verses are Paul's instructions that *all* (men and women, rich and poor, the spiritual and the not-so-spiritual) should be allowed to bring a hymn, word of instruction, a revelation, etc., and contain his warning that women should not be silenced. The process of who should be allowed to speak and when must not be controlled by the male leaders. If someone has a word "from the floor," they should be allowed to speak and not silenced. The Corinthian leaders are not to worry that there will be general chaos as everyone will take it in turns, prophecies will be weighed, the spirits of the prophets are subject to the control of the prophets, and God is not a God of disorder but of peace.

What then shall we say brothers? When you come together, everyone has a hymn, or a word of instruction, a revelation, a tongue, or an interpretation. All of these must be done for the strengthening of the church. If anyone speaks in a tongue, two—or at the most three—should speak, one at a time, and someone must interpret. If there is no interpreter, the speaker should keep quiet in the church and speak to himself and God. Two or three prophets should speak, and the others should weigh carefully what is said. And if a revelation comes to someone who is sitting down, the first speaker should stop. For you can all prophesy in turn so that everyone may be instructed and encouraged. The spirits of the prophets are subject to the control of the prophets. For God is not a God of disorder but of peace.

As in all the congregations of the saints, women should remain silent in the churches. They are not allowed to speak, but must be in submission, as the Law says. If they want to enquire about something they should ask their own husbands at home; for it is disgraceful for a woman to speak in the church.

Did the word of God originate with you? Or are you the only ones it has reached? If anybody thinks he is a prophet or spiritually gifted, let him acknowledge that what I am writing to you is the Lord's command. If he ignores this, he himself will be ignored. Therefore, my brothers, be eager to prophesy, and do not forbid speaking in tongues. But everything should be done in a fitting and orderly way.

Bibliography

Adams, Edward, and David Horrell. "Scholarly Quest for Paul's Church at Corinth." In *Christianity at Corinth: The Quest for the Pauline Church*, edited by Edward Adams and David G. Horrell, 1–43. Louisville, KY: Westminster John Knox, 2004.

Allison, R. W. "'Let the Women Be Silent in the Churches,' (1 Cor 14:33b–36): What Did Paul Really Say, and What Did It Mean?" *Journal for the Study of the New Testament* 32 (1988) 27–60.

Barclay, William. *The Letter to the Corinthians*. Edinburgh: St. Andrew, 2002.

Barrett, C. K. *A Commentary on The First Epistle to the Corinthians*. London: A & C Black, 1971.

Barth, Karl. *The Resurrection of the Dead*. Translated by H. J. Stenning. London: Hodder & Stoughton, 1933.

Blomberg, Craig. *The NIV Application Commentary: I Corinthians*. Grand Rapids: Zondervan, 1994.

Bristow, John Temple. *What Paul Really Said about Women: An Apostle's Liberating Views on Equality in Marriage, Leadership, and Love*. New York: HarperOne, 1988.

Caird, George B. "Paul and Women's Liberty." *Bulletin of the John Rylands Library of Manchester* 54 (1972) 268–81.

Campbell, Douglas A. *The Deliverance of God: An Apocalyptic Rereading of Justification in Paul*. Grand Rapids: Eerdmans, 2009.

———. *The Quest for Paul's Gospel: A Suggested Strategy*. London: T & T Clark, 2005.

Chrysostom, John. *Homilies on the Epistles of Paul to the Corinthians*. NPNF 1–14. Edited by Philip Schaff. Edinburgh: T & T Clark, 1889.

Clement. "The First Epistle of Clement to the Corinthians." In *The Apostolic Fathers: Early Christian Writings*, rev. ed., edited by Andrew Louth and translated by Maxwell Staniforth, 23–51. London: Penguin, 1968.

Dempster, Stephen D. *Dominion and Dynasty: A Theology of the Hebrew Bible*. Downers Grove, IL: IVP, 2003.

Edsall, Benjamin A. "Greco-Roman Costume and Paul's Fraught Argument in 1 Corinthians 11.2–16." *Journal of Greco-Roman Christianity and Judaism* 9 (2013) 132–46.

Erdman, C. R. *The First Epistle of Paul to the Corinthians: An Exposition*. Grand Rapids: Baker, 1966.

Fee, Gordon E. *The First Epistle to the Corinthians*. Grand Rapids: Eerdmans, 1991.

Finney, Mark. "Honour, Head-coverings and Headship: 1 Corinthians 11.2–16 in its Social Context." *Journal for the Study of the New Testament* 33.1 (2010) 31–58.

Fitzmyer, Joseph A. *First Corinthians*. New Haven: Yale University Press, 2008.

Flanagan, N. M., and E. H. Snyder. "Did Paul Put Down Women in 1 Cor 14:34–36?" *Biblical Theology Bulletin* 11 (1981) 10–12.

Glen, Stanley J. *Pastoral Problems in First Corinthians*. London: Epworth, 1965.

Grosheide, F. W. *Commentary on the First Epistle to the Corinthians: The English Text with Introduction, Exposition and Notes*. Grand Rapids: Eerdmans, 1953.

Grudem, W. A. "1 Cor 14:20–25: Prophecy and Tongues as Signs of God's Attitude." *Westminster Theological Journal* 41 (1979) 381–96.

Gundry-Volf, J. M. "Gender and Creation in 1 Cor 11:2–16: A Study in Paul's Theological Method." In *Evangelium, Schriftauslegung, Kirche: Festschrift für P. Stuhlmacher*, edited by J. Adna, S. J. Hafeman, and O. Hofius, 151–71. Göttingen: Vandenhoeck & Ruprecht, 1997.

Habets, Myk, and Beulah Wood, eds. *Reconsidering Gender: Evangelical Perspectives*. Eugene, OR: Pickwick, 2011.

Hays, Richard B. *First Corinthians*. Louisville, KY: John Knox, 1997.

Héring, Jean. *The First Epistle of Saint Paul to the Corinthians*. London: Epworth, 1962.

Hodge, Charles. *An Exposition of the First Epistle to the Corinthians*. London: Banner of Truth, 1959.

Holmberg, Bengt. "Methods of Historical Reconstruction." In *Christianity at Corinth: The Quest for the Pauline Church*, edited by Edward Adams and David G. Horrell, 255–71. Louisville, KY: Westminster John Knox, 2004.

Horrell, David G. *The Social Ethos of the Corinthian Correspondence: Interests and Ideology from 1 Corinthians to 1 Clement*. Edinburgh: T & T Clark, 1996.

Horsley, Richard A. *1 Corinthians*. Nashville: Abingdon, 1998.

———. "Wisdom of Word and Words of Wisdom in Corinth." *Catholic Biblical Quarterly* 39 (1977) 224–39.

Hurd, John Coolidge, Jr. *The Origin of 1 Corinthians*. Macon, GA: Mercer University Press, 1983.

Hurley, J. B. "Did Paul Require Veils or the Silence of Women? A Consideration of 1 Cor 11:2–16 and 1 Cor 14:33b–36." *Westminster Theological Journal* 35 (1973) 190–220.

Johanson, B. C. "Tongues, a Sign for Unbelievers?: A Structural and Exegetical Study of 1 Corinthians XIV.20–25." *New Testament Studies* 25 (1979) 180–203.

Johnson, Alan F. *1 Corinthians*. Downers Grove, IL: IVP, 2004.

Jüngel, Eberhard. *God as the Mystery of the World*. Translated by Darrell L. Guder. Edinburgh: T & T Clark, 1983.

Kaiser, W. C. "Paul, Women, and the Church." *Worldwide Challenge* 3 (1976) 9–12.

Kennedy, G. A. *The Art of Rhetoric in the Roman World*. Princeton: Princeton University Press, 1972.

Kovacs, Judith L., ed. *1 Corinthians: Interpreted by Early Christian Commentators*. Translated by Judith L. Kovacs. Grand Rapids: Eerdmans, 2005.

Kroeger, Richard Clark, and Catherine Clark Kroeger. *I Suffer Not a Woman: Rethinking 1 Timothy 2:11–15 in Light of Ancient Evidence*. Grand Rapids: Baker Academic, 1992.

Lakey, Michael J. *Image and Glory of God: 1 Corinthians 11:2–16 as a Case Study in Bible, Gender and Hermeneutics*. London: T & T Clark, 2010.

Lanier, D. E. "With Stammering Lips and Another Tongue: 1 Cor 14:20–22 and Isa 28:11–12." *Criswell Theological Review* 5 (1991) 259–85.

Llewellyn-Jones, Lloyd. *Aphrodite's Tortoise: The Veiled Woman of Ancient Greece*. Swansea, UK: Classical Press of Wales, 2003.

Louth, Andrew, ed. *The Apostolic Fathers: Early Christian Writings*. Translated by Maxwell Staniforth. London: Penguin, 1968.

Macaskill, Grant. *Union with Christ in the New Testament*. Oxford: Oxford University Press, 2013.

MacDonald, Margaret. *The Pauline Churches*. Cambridge: Cambridge University Press, 1988.

Manus, C. U. "The Subordination of Women in the Church: 1 Cor 14:33b–36 Reconsidered." *Review of African Theology* 8 (1984) 183–95.

Martin, Dale. *The Corinthian Body*. New Haven: Yale University Press, 1995.

Martin, T. W. "Paul's Argument from Nature for the Veil in 1 Corinthians 11:13–15: A Testicle Instead of a Head Covering." *Journal of Biblical Literature* 123 (2004) 75–84.

Martin, W. J. "1 Cor 11:2–16: An Interpretation." In *Apostolic History and the Gospel: Presented to F. F. Bruce*, edited by W. Ward Gasque and R. P. Martin, 231–41. Exeter, UK: Paternoster, 1970.

Meeks, Wayne, A. "The Image of the Androgyne: Some Uses of Symbol in Earliest Christianity." *History of Religions* 13.3 (1974) 165–208.

———. *The Writings of St. Paul*. New York: Norton/Scribners, 1972.

Moffatt, J. *First Epistle of Paul to the Corinthians*. London: Hodder & Stoughton, 1938.

Moule, C. F. D. *Worship in the New Testament*. London: Lutterworth, 1961.

Murphy-O'Connor, Jerome. *Keys to First Corinthians: Revisiting the Major Issues*. Oxford: Oxford University Press, 2009.

Odell-Scott, D. W. "In Defence of an Egalitarian Interpretation of 1 Cor 14:34–36." *Biblical Theology Bulletin* 17 (1987) 100–103.

———. "Let the Women Speak in Church: An Egalitarian Interpretation of 1 Cor 14:33b–36." *Biblical Theology Bulletin* 13 (1983) 90–93.

O'Loughlin, Tom. "Why Study the Early Eucharist?" http://www.youtube.com/watch?v=oSN2r4gP5-o&feature=youtu.be (accessed Feb. 7, 2014).

Olson, Kelly. *Dress and the Roman Woman: Self-Presentation and Society*. London: Routledge, 2008.

Oster, R. E. "Use, Misuse and Neglect of Archaeological Evidence in Some Modern Works on 1 Corinthians (1 Cor 7:1–5; 8:10; 11:2–16; 12:14–26)." *Zeitschrift für die neutestamentliche Wissenschaft und die Kunde der älteren Kirche* 83 (1992) 52–73.

Padgett, Alan G. *As Christ Submits to the Church: A Biblical Understanding of Leadership and Mutual Submission*. Grand Rapids: Baker Academic, 2011.

Paige, Terence. "Stoicism, ἐλευθερία and Community at Corinth." In *Christianity at Corinth: The Quest for the Pauline Church*, edited by Edward Adams and David G. Horrell, 207–18. Louisville, KY: Westminster John Knox, 2004.

Payne, Philip B. *Man and Woman, One in Christ: An Exegetical and Theological Study of Paul's Letters*. Grand Rapids: Zondervan, 2009.

———. "Wild Hair and Gender Equality in 1 Corinthians 11:2–16." *Priscilla Papers* 20.3 (2006) 9–18.

Peirce, Charles S. *Selected Writings: Values in a Universe of Chance*, edited by Philip P. Weiner. New York: Dover, 1958.

Peterson, Trevor. "The Use of Isa 28:11–12 in 1 Cor 14:20–22." Unpublished paper, December 11, 1996. 12 pages. Online: http://www.scribd.com/doc/128105660/The-Use-of-Isa-28-11-12-in-1-Cor-14 (accessed 30th Nov., 2013).

Phillips, J. B. *The New Testament in Modern English*. Pocket ed. London: Geoffrey Bles, 1960.

Prior, David. *The Message of 1 Corinthians*. Leicester, UK: IVP, 1985.

Robertson, A., and A. Plummer. *A Critical and Exegetical Commentary on the First Epistle of St. Paul to the Corinthians*. Edinburgh: T & T Clark, 1914.

Roberts, P. "A Sign—Christian or Pagan?" *Expository Times* 90 (1979) 199–203.

Rose, Margaret A. *Parody: Ancient, Modern, and Post-Modern*. Cambridge: Cambridge University Press, 1993.

Richards, E. Randolph. *Paul and First-Century Letter Writing: Secretaries, Composition and Collection*. Downers Grove, IL: IVP, 2004.

Schüssler Fiorenza, E. *In Memory of Her: A Feminist Theological Reconstruction of Christian Origins*. London: SCM, 1983.

Shoemaker, Thomas P. "Unveiling of Equality: 1 Corinthians 11:2–16." *Biblical Theology Bulletin* 17 (1987) 60–63.

Stanley, C. D. *Paul and the Language of Scripture: Citation Technique in the Pauline Epistles and Contemporary Literature*. Cambridge: Cambridge University Press, 2008.

Terry, Bruce. "'No Such Custom': An Exposition of 1 Corinthians 11:2–16." Online: http://www.the-highway.com/no-such-custom_Terry.html (accessed 25 October 2012).

Tertullian. *Treatises on Penance: On Penitence and On Purity*. Ancient Christian Writers 28. New York: Paulist, 1959.

Thiselton, Anthony. *First Corinthians: A Shorter Exegetical and Pastoral Commentary*. New International Greek Testament Commentaries. Grand Rapids: Eerdmans, 2006.

———. *The First Epistle to the Corinthians*. Grand Rapids: Eerdmans, 2000.

Vadakkedom, Jose. "The Letter of Corinthians to Paul the Apostle." *Bible Bhashayam* 34.4 (2008) 273–97.

Walker, William O. *Interpolations in the Pauline Letters*. London: Sheffield Academic Press, 2001.

Winter, Bruce W. *After Paul Left Corinth: The Influence of Secular Ethics and Social Change*. Grand Rapids: Eerdmans, 2001.

Wire, A. C. *The Corinthian Women Prophets: A Reconstruction through Paul's Rhetoric*. Minneapolis: Fortress, 1990.

Witherington III, Ben. *Conflict and Community in Corinth: A Socio-Rhetorical Commentary on 1 and 2 Corinthians*. Grand Rapids: Eerdmans, 1995.

Wright, N. T. *Colossians and Philemon*. Tyndale New Testament Commentaries. Leicester, UK: IVP, 1986.

———. *Paul and the Faithfulness of God*. London: SPCK, 2013.

Name Index